M000035504

"A piercing, sharpening, honest appraisal of the spiritual and practical necessities of church planting and the church planter. Michael Crawford offers a straight-talking encyclopedia of the good, bad, and ugly of church planting. Every potential church planter should read this book for a heart-check before plunging into the deep end of this critical calling. Every present and past church planter should read it for a gut-check and a head-check, as they continue in whatever phase of the church's life they find themselves. An important read for anyone leading or participating at any phase of a new church's conception, birth, growth, or decline."

—**BRIAN LOPICCOLO** founding pastor of Deep Run Church, MD

Michael Crawford is an extraordinary leader and gift to the church. He has had an immeasurable impact on my life and on the lives of countless others. He is a consistent source of wisdom and contrarian thinking. I have been immensely blessed by his wisdom and writing. I highly commend this book to you. Read it and re-read it!

—**BRIAN HOWARD** Vice President of the U.S. Networks for Acts 29

Great book . . . I keep seeing one-liners that make me have to resist the urge to re-activate my twitter account so I can post quotes. Overflowing with practical wisdom that has DEPTH. Going to take the next month and just do what is said in Chapter 12.

—**JAMES TYLER** Pastor of Grace Baptist Church, Papillon, NE

Don't Plant—Be Planted is the Ecclesiastes for church planters. Like firmly embedded nails of seasoned wisdom, Michael Crawford's contrarian reflections and exhortations about church planting are a must-have for any prospective church planter, church planting team and movement leaders. The bottom line gospel goads given cut through a lot of hype about church planting and can save leaders a ton from wasteful pretenses. I wish I had it decades ago.

—**CRAIG GARRIOTT** Baltimore Antioch Leadership Movement

I loved this book. While reading it I found myself affirming Crawford's views concerning the family's call, women's role in ministry, and pastors getting paid . . . *out loud*. I definitely want to use this with every planter (and pastor) that we send out.

—JAMIE CALDWELL Lead Pastor of Redemption Church, MD

It is rare to find a book on starting churches that is so biblically grounded while at the same time so real and practical. Michael is a practitioner. Though the thoughts are compelling, nothing he shares in this book is mere theory but has been tested upon the difficult grounds of real urban church planting. Michael is a leader of leaders and I'm thankful that those interested in the endeavor of planting churches will benefit from his wisdom.

—DAN HYUN SEND City Missionary

DON'T PLANT

PLANT

BE PLANTED

CONTRARIAN OBSERVATIONS ABOUT STARTING A CHURCH

DON'T PLANT

BE PLANTED

CONTRARIAN OBSERVATIONS ABOUT STARTING A CHURCH

MICHAEL CRAWFORD

SQUARE HALO BOOKS

In Christian art, the square halo identified a living person presumed to be a saint. Square Halo Books is devoted to publishing works that present contextually sensitive biblical studies, and practical instruction consistent with the Doctrines of the Reformation. The goal of Square Halo Books is to provide materials useful for encouraging and equipping the saints.

©2019 Square Halo Books, Inc.
P.O. Box 18954
Baltimore, MD 21206
www.SquareHaloBooks.com

ISBN 978-1-941106-12-9
Library of Congress Control Number: 2019954030

Printed in the United States of America

*I am writing this book
particularly to potential
and current church planters.
Though I hope that any reader
of this book is blessed by it,
my peculiar prayer is that
those of you who are in
or entering the violent and
volatile world of church planting
will find my words a
helpful guide to your soul.*

Join me in the journey.

CONTENTS

00

PREFACE

This book is written as a guide to *you*—whoever you are and whatever your connection to church planting. I've written this book in a conversational style so that it imitates what it might be like for you if I were sitting across the table from you discussing your ministry. The majority of the chapters are extended reflections on key topics related to church planting. Interspersed between these longer reflections are several short chapters, these are supposed to be pondered more than understood. Let these provoke you to thought. Though each chapter is largely independent of the others, the book is arranged in strategic order and I recommend reading it as it has been laid out here.

THINKING

Thinking is soul shaping. This book was written to get you to think. You are going to find this book controversial at points, and that is intended to provoke you toward thought. Controversy is useful insofar as it leads to an increase in clarity. This book is a contrarian guide not for the sake of controversy alone, but for the sake of your transformation.

One of the most soul shaping experiences of my fifty-plus years of life was interacting with Dr. Frazier at the Master's College. His main purpose as the head of the political studies department was to get kids to think. He helped me to think critically and analytically, and my approach in this book is heavily influenced by my experience with him. The danger with any movement or system is that after we accomplish our objectives, we arrive, and stop thinking. The very thinking that delivered this new thing—with all its wonder and promise—ceases to exist. This is a danger for church planting.

As planting has become somewhat popular - and there are multiple systems out there—we face the temptation to stop thinking and repeat the past. But, God is always up to something new. *Redemptive history is a case study of the ingenuity of God.* A lot of what I am going to say in the coming chapters that seems contrarian is just biblical. It's only contrarian because it's contrary to what many of us are thinking and doing. He is not afraid to do new things and we need to be aware of that.

EPISTEMOLOGY

It is also necessary to say a word about epistemology. When it comes to church planting, you have to ask yourself, who or what is your final authority? How do you know what you should think, believe, and do? That question is an ever-present challenge for us. At the end of the day, is our authority going to be Scripture or our experiences? Scripture or our successes? Scripture or our systems? I answer those questions with the conviction that the closer we can get to understanding what the Bible says and even emulating some of the Bible's church planting methodologies, the better off we will be. I write unashamedly with an epistemology that sees the sixty-six books of the Bible as the purest and most authoritative source of God's instruction to His Church.

This book is written with an earnest desire to see Scripture reigning supreme over every bit of what we do in church planting. I also acknowledge that the same Holy Spirit that inspired the Scriptures has been at work in the Church and in the saints throughout the ages, and that there are insights to be learned from those who have gone before us.[1] But I believe that we (and our church plants) should bleed like John Bunyan: with Scripture.[2]

MY STORY

My own story (see Chapter One) has a level of contrarianism to it. I didn't grow up in a Christian home. I wasn't converted through an evangelistic movement, gifted preacher, or step by step tract. I moved from the West Coast to the East Coast to plant. I planted at an older than average age. On top of all these things, my planting methodology wasn't typical. When I moved to Baltimore to plant Freedom Church, I quickly realized that my planting paradigm of *planting myself, planting my family, and then planting a church* (see Chapter Twenty-Eight) was a contrarian way to church plant. Some people questioned my approach, but I felt convicted to work in that order. God has often taken me against the grain of the present Christian culture, and much of my approach has been forged by seeing Him work with me in unusual ways. My own story certainly shapes the way I think about church planting, and my thoughts in this book sprouted out of my own ongoing experience as a planter and with the many planters I have counseled.

A FRIEND

Another huge influence on what follows in this book is my friend Ronnie Martin, pastor of Substance Church in Ashland and Wooster, Ohio. Ronnie has challenged me to consider how I approach things. He is not afraid to ask a crazy question, to say "what if?" and to explore. We typically use only a couple of strategies in church planting, but Ronnie is quick to remind me that God has an abundance of strategies. He doesn't lock God into a church planting box. Ronnie has helped me to think creatively and imaginatively, and our conversations have left a lasting impact on the way I view church planting.

01

MY STORY

When [Jesus] came down from the mountain, great crowds followed him. And behold, a leper came to him and knelt before him, saying, "Lord, if you will, you can make me clean." And Jesus stretched out his hand and touched him, saying, "I will; be clean." And immediately his leprosy was cleansed.—Matthew 8:1–3

If not for these three verses, I wouldn't be alive.

I was born in 1968 in Los Angeles as the youngest of eight siblings. I had a fairly normal childhood except that my mom was a single mother. Growing up, I never went to a church, never read a Bible, and don't recall ever meeting a Christian or hearing about Christianity. When I was nine years old, my mother got a job taking care of a house in Malibu, so we moved there. In Malibu, I met some Jewish kids who didn't know much about Judaism, but I still had no contact with Christians.

In high school one of my brothers became a Christian, and started talking about Jesus a lot. I remember that my family, me in particular, was afraid of him and what had happened to him. I knew that whatever had gotten hold of him could get in the way of my Malibu dreams of becoming rich and successful.

In high school, I also met and fell in love with a girl who was white and Jewish and her parents didn't allow us to date because I was black. The event deeply wounded me and sent me into a spiral of anger and disillusionment. Rap music became the outlet for my pain. Rap music became a form of protest for me. I actually became a rapper, formed a group, performed, and started making albums. Though I had some success, my dreams eventually fell apart. We thought we were going to get a record deal, but things fell through and that sent me back into depression.

My mother noticed what was going on with me and decided to take me to a psychiatrist. The psychiatrist told me to do the two things that had gotten me into my mess: go get a white girlfriend and keep doing rap music. That advice seemed irrational and illogical to me. I could not imagine why I would do the same things that caused me to be depressed to heal me. I also observed that the majority of people coming out of the psychiatrists office didn't seem to be getting any better. The psychiatrist didn't have a solution for me.

At this point, my despair reached a climax. I decided that I was going to take my life. I went out to the beach to plot out how I was going to kill myself, and it was on the beach that God told me, "Go get a Bible." Obviously, at the time, I didn't know who or what was speaking to me, but it became apparent later on. I drove to a bookstore and asked the staff for a Bible. I remember telling them that I wanted a Bible where I could know what Jesus said because my brother was always talking about Jesus's words.

I searched through the Bible until I found the red letters. I was still planning to kill myself, however. So my thinking was, "I'm going to read these red letters and then I'm going to kill myself and that way, when I die, and God asks 'Why should I let you into heaven?' I'm going to tell Him, 'Because I read the Bible.'"

What happened instead was that I began reading the red letters, I fell in love with Jesus, and the Holy Spirit came and breathed life into my soul. I was saved in the summer of 1987, in my bedroom, weeping as I read the red letters of a King James Bible. I was particularly impacted by the story of the leper in Matthew 8 and the paralytic in Matthew 9. God showed me that He could forgive all my wickedness and heal the leprosy in my soul.

After I got saved the majority of my desires changed, but I had no idea what to do with myself. There weren't any Christians around me, I didn't have a church and I didn't have a small group or a Bible study to attend. I just got saved. As God began to work His transformation in my life, my mom got even more worried about me because she saw that I no longer wanted to party and do the things that I used to do. So, she called her boss' architect, Joe Weezer, whom she knew was a Christian, and asked him to come sort me out. What she didn't know is that he was from Grace Community Church, the church where John MacArthur pastors. When Joe found out what had happened to me he got excited. He took me to Grace, where I was baptized.

The first time I went to church at Grace—which was the first time I had ever been to church in my eighteen years of life—I cried when I heard John

MacArthur preach. I didn't know the meaning of my emotions, but Joe Weezer did; he knew that God was calling me to preach. Joe asked me, "Do you want to do that?" I was unsure, but he told me that I could learn.

So God called me into the ministry very early on in my Christian life. I was discipled by a bunch of great young men, and eventually enrolled at the Masters College, where I received more theological training. But my plan was to go on to law school, not full-time ministry. I didn't think the Church could handle a preacher like me who wasn't Christianized and who was willing to say exactly what the Bible said, no matter what. God altered my plans, however, and I continued on to graduate studies at the Master's Seminary.

During my time in seminary, God began to lay on me a passion to go to an inner city that had a large population of African Americans, but this desire wouldn't be realized until much later. After seminary, I pastored a church for almost twenty years in the Antelope Valley of California. As I got older, my calling to an inner city became clearer and clearer. In 2008, God made it plain that the church I was pastoring was no longer the place for me, so I began the transition process.

After that, one of the churches I had helped to start called me and said they wanted me to be their missions pastor for six months because they believed that God was going to send me to an inner city. I became the missions pastor at Cornerstone Bible Church in Ridgecrest, California, where they affirmed my calling, laid hands on me, and partnered with other churches to send me out to Baltimore, Maryland.

Originally I thought there was no way that Baltimore would be where I would church plant. I told my wife the day before our visit to Baltimore that God was going to have to speak to me in a mighty way to take us there. As soon as I landed, though, I knew. When we drove past downtown on I-95 I began to weep, and the Spirit of God confirmed that this was where I needed to be. I went through assessments with several churches and organizations, which affirmed my calling to "Charm City." God provided in miraculous ways. For example, the housing market was upside down and moving was exceptionally difficult, but pieces came together that allowed us to afford the move.

God already had a man named Rob Steinbach living a mile and a half from where we settled. Rob had a vision to see a church started in his children's school. Rob was elder qualified, and I knew I did not want to plant alone. So, through prayer and fasting, Rob and I discerned that it was God's intent for us to join together to plant a church. God began to pool people together and we had a core group in place much earlier than I had planned. In January of 2010 we officially launched Freedom Church.

I still serve as one of the pastors of Freedom Church. Also, I have worked as the interim director of missions for Maryland and Delaware, and am deeply involved in church planting efforts in Baltimore. I have spent my whole adult life living and working in the Church, and the majority of the last decade planting churches and training, equipping, and coaching other church planters. I also work for the NAMB (north American missions board) and (bcmd) as the State Director of Mission for the Baptist Convention of Maryland and Delaware overseeing church planting.

I tell you all this to give you a window into who I am, and to make it clear that I am your fellow companion on the journey of following Jesus as He builds His Church and fills the earth with the knowledge of the glory of His name. I'm still learning and still being sanctified, and I pray that God uses some of what He has taught me to teach and shape you.

02

CHURCH PLANTING: A CALLING OR AN OPPORTUNITY?

There is a difference between a calling and an opportunity. The call to plant a church is not an opportunity. An opportunity is an option to do something. A call is entirely different; it is when God tells you to do something—and when God tells you to do something, you must obey. You have an opportunity to plant a church when there is a job available, money available, training available, a city to plant in, and assessments to pass. These are good and important things, but their presence does not necessarily mean that you have a calling.

Consider a few examples of calling in Scripture. The first calling in the Bible was to Adam. God told him exactly what to do: be fruitful and multiply, have dominion, avoid the tree of the knowledge of good and evil. The second calling was to Noah. God told Noah, "Build this boat, these are the specs, here is what is going to happen." Then there is Abraham. Abraham is the prototypical church planter: he is called to leave his place, to go to another place, to reach a people, and to create a place and a people. That is the essence of church planting, and Abraham is the first one in history to do it. Abraham's call was very clear and it came from God—God told him exactly what to do.

So what does it mean for God to tell someone to plant a church? Can God still speak like He did to Adam, Noah, and Abraham? And if so, how does He do it? I believe that He does, and if that is true then one of the first questions you must ask yourself as a church planter or potential planter is whether or not God has spoken like this to you. Has God called you to plant a church?

GOD SPEAKING

Of course, answering that question is much more complex than asking it. If God is going to tell you to plant a church, it is important for you to know how He might do that. Consider these three ways:

1. THROUGH THE WRITTEN WORD OF GOD

God calls people through Scripture—the sixty-six books. As you work through the pages of Scripture, God may say to you, "I want you to do that" or "I want you to do something like what they did." The Bible gives us illustration after illustration of people receiving callings from God. As you read through the biblical narrative, you may identify with and relate to certain people and situations in the text. Pay attention to those. If God has spoken in a certain way in the past, we can expect that He might speak the same way again, and He might be doing so to you. Scripture lets us know what callings sound like and enables us to hear one when it comes our way. The word of God is living, and God often calls through it. Scripture is constantly shaping us as we read it, and for some of you, it will shape you into a church planter and call you into that vocation.

2. THROUGH THE LOCAL CHURCH

God has a proclivity for speaking to people through the local church. What this means is that when a church says something like, "God gave us a commission to go and to make disciples and to gather disciples of Jesus into churches," and "We believe that it is God's will for someone among us to go do that." God may use that message to call a planter. Let me be clear: churches have no place calling someone to do something that God hasn't called them to do—that is dangerous territory. But God has given a particular authority to the local church, and we should not be surprised if He uses a local church to deliver messages that actually come from Him. So be attentive to your community of faith, as this might be how God is calling or has already called you.

3. THROUGH THE HOLY SPIRIT DIRECTLY TO YOU

Communication happens between God's Spirit and our spirit. The Bible says that, " The Spirit himself bears witness with our spirit that we are children of God" (Romans 8:16). Further, a sound theology of the Holy Spirit recognizes Him as a person, not a thing or a force. It would be crazy to expect the personal and relational Holy Spirit, who dwells within Christians, to remain silent. We should expect some Holy Spirit-to-person communication to go on in the life of a Christian. And, if we take some hints from the book of Acts we should also expect that when the Holy Spirit indwells men and women He is apt to tell some people to go plant churches.

God can call you to plant a church through direct communication from the Holy Spirit. Admittedly, the exact nature of this communication is much harder to put a finger on. Whether you sense it as an inner voice, a feeling you can't get away from, or a thought that keeps coming across your mind—I don't know exactly what it will be like for you—there is a good chance that these things are actually God speaking to you. You need to be open to this possibility and listening for God to call you in this manner, if He so wills.

This may rub up against your theology of spiritual gifts, but let me say this: the exaggerations of this doctrine are not good reasons to deny it. The abuses of this—all the unfounded "God told me's"—are not good reasons to deny it. Now, I would be shocked if someone said, "I heard an audible voice and the audible voice told me to go plant a church." Typically, God uses an audible voice on rare occasions and usually these are huge moments in human history. When God talks out loud it's a big deal. I hate to bust our significance bubbles, but He rarely does it and I'm a little suspicious of those types of claims.

As a general rule, if you feel like God's Spirit has communicated to you that you should plant a church, you shouldn't spend too much time questioning that. Who's going to tell you to do that? Satan's not going to tell you to do that—Satan is going to tell you to do things that violate the Word, not obey it. Who else would tell you to plant a church other than God?

YOU HEARING

The other half of God speaking to you is you hearing Him and discerning what He said. This can be incredibly difficult. Here are some ways to discern your calling:

I. HAVE A REAL RELATIONSHIP WITH GOD

As we've already established, this is vital because in a relationship there is communication. If you spend enough time with God I can't see how you're going to miss a calling from Him. God has never had a problem communicating what He wants us to do. He has never had a problem making something clear. Ever. So, if God wants you to know something, and you have made yourself available to Him, I don't think anything is going to stop Him. This also means that if you are in real relationship with God and you don't know what God wants you to do yet or you aren't sure if He is calling you to something, that is probably because He hasn't shown you yet. Once God wants you to know, you're going to know. If you doubt that, read the book of Jonah.

Having a real relationship with God also implies that you have a real and regular relationship with scripture. An important implication of this is that you should be able to see your calling in the Bible—it should be in conformity to biblical principles and should have at least some resemblance to a calling in the biblical record. If you cannot root your calling in the Bible then it is not a calling. Practically, that means you should be able to connect the dots from the first book of Genesis to you and your plant, and see how you fit in with what God is doing and has been doing throughout history.

2. HAVE A REAL RELATIONSHIP WITH A LOCAL CHURCH

Not just any local church, but a church committed to the biblical qualifications for pastors and planters. A church that studies and is familiar with the nature of biblical callings, and has experience with pastoring others through the discernment of callings. Paul got his call outside of the local church, but it was confirmed and clarified in the local church. In Galatians 2, Paul says the church "saw that I had been entrusted with the gospel to the uncircumcised, just as Peter had been entrusted with the gospel to the circumcised" (v7). The church basically said, "Yep, he's got it. We've seen it before in Peter." In the New Covenant, the local church is the clarifier and commissioner of the call of God. You're going to need the wisdom and input of the institution against which God promised the gates of hell would not prevail. If you sense a calling to church plant, you've got to ask your church: "Do you see Titus 1 and 1 Timothy 3 in me? Do you see God working in me and calling me? And if you do, are you willing to lay hands on me and affirm it?"

3. GET THE INPUT OF REALLY GOOD FRIENDS

When I say really good friends, I'm talking about people who know you— who really know you. You need to talk to the kind of people who will tell you when you're wrong. Take your calling before others and ask them if they can see it. We all have blind spots and "in an abundance of counselors there is safety" (Proverbs 11:14). Make sure you consult those who have had the most experience with you.

A WORD ABOUT PROVIDENCE

In God's providence you may have the opportunity to plant a church before you, but I want to reiterate that just because you have an opportunity to plant a church doesn't mean you are called to do so. Providence is just where you find yourself in the present tense, and we call it God's providence because we believe that He is sovereign. If I visit a job search website, in God's providence I'm exposed to a million job opportunities, but that doesn't mean I'm called to any of them. Providence can put you in a place where you have choices, but that is not a call.

On the flip side—note the nuance here—when God calls, the providences follow. Example? Moses. He was walking one day and in the providence of God he ran into a burning bush. The voice from the bush called him. His calling came from an unusually providential moment. Providences should support your call. You can't find a guy in Scripture who was called and had no providences to back up his call, and most of the time there is a supernatural element to the providences. God called Abraham to go up the mountain and sacrifice, and when God called out to him to stop, in God's providence there was a ram in the bushes. So, if you say you've been called to plant a church but there are no providential happenings to support your call—like financial support or a core team of members—you need to consider the authenticity, or, at least timing of your calling.

I'm not saying that everything has to fall in place or be perfect. We all want a burning bush, but it's usually not that easy. Romans 4 tells us that in following His call from God, Abraham had to believe against hope. (4:18). Abraham didn't see a realistic opportunity to have offspring, and He thought God's providence had led him to a place where the promise could no longer come true. But even in this case, the providences did eventually follow. Sarah got pregnant and Isaac was born. So, if you feel like you're trying to discern whether or not you have been called to plant a church, you need to be looking out for providences that support your calling. You're not going to get a handwritten note from God telling you exactly what to do, but you will likely get some strong hints from God. On the other side, if you are experiencing a number of inexplicable providences that you haven't linked to a calling from God, you ought to consider whether God might be waking you up to something—maybe you are missing His voice.

A SOURCE OF CONFUSION

Money can produce a lot of confusion in all this, and it can lead to distortion of your calling. This becomes especially dangerous when money is only available for certain types of church plants (i.e inner-city churches, house churches, or suburban churches). If a network or organization is only funding certain types of callings, then that can bring a lot of temptation and distraction to you as you are trying to discern the specifics of your calling. If you know God has called you to plant a church in a city, but you're not exactly sure where and you only have the potential to be funded if you plant within certain limits, then it is going to be much harder for you to hear God if He is directing you to a type of plant that doesn't qualify for funding. Let this be a note to those of us who are leaders in church planting networks and denominations: we need to be aware of the multitude of ways that God calls people and be prepared to support individuals in whatever God wants to do. As a planter, you need to be on guard against the pull of the flesh to follow the dollar.

CLARITY

An Acts 29 Network pastor once said to me years ago that God always calls you to a people and a place. I think you can trace that out biblically. So if you know God has called you to plant a church, and you have begun to discern where He wants you to plant and some of the details of your calling, then you are in a thrilling and terrifying position. That means that planting is not just an opportunity for you—it's a calling. And if planting is calling to you from God, then that has major implications. We always say, "God, I want you to make this clear," but the majority of time when God tells us to do something we don't do it anyway. Clarity does not necessarily help us to obey, but it just gives us something clearly to disobey. Clarity raises the stakes for our obedience! So if church planting really is a calling for you, it's not optional. You've got to go do it.

A DIVERSITY OF BIBLICAL CALLINGS

Most of us are familiar with the callings of Adam, Noah, Abraham, and other big name Bible characters, but there are many more callings in Scripture to learn from. Several of these callings that you may not know as well are listed below. Note the diversity of ways that God calls—God might be calling you in ways you don't even think are possible. God has used and continues to use a diversity of means to deliver callings.

JACOB

Genesis 31:3 "Return to the land of your fathers and to your kindred, and I will be with you." God speaks to Jacob through a dream. He says that He has seen all that Laban is doing to Jacob (attempting to cheat him out of wages, etc.) and that He is sending Jacob back home.

BARAK

Judges 4:6 "Go, gather your men at Mount Tabor, taking ten thousand from the people of Naphtali and the people of Zebulun." God gives order to Barak through Deborah, a prophetess, to gather an army of men and overtake their enemy, the king of Canaan. ". . . So the Lord sold them into the hands of Jabin . . ." (v. 1–3)

ESTHER

Esther 4:8 "To go into the king's presence to beg for mercy and plead with him for her people." God inspires a holy distress in Esther over what was happening to the Jews. This distress leads her to the conviction that she must go before the king—risking almost certain death—and plead for mercy.

EZEKIEL

Ezekiel 2:4–8 "Say to them, 'Thus says the Lord God.' And whether they hear or refuse to hear (for they are a rebellious house) they will know that a prophet has been among them. And you, son of man, be not afraid of them, nor be afraid of their words, though briers and thorns are with you and you sit on scorpions. Be not afraid of their words . . . Be not rebellious like that rebellious house." In a vision, God tells Ezekiel that He will be sending him to proclaim God's word to the rebellious Israelites.

STEPHEN

Acts 6:2–4 "And the twelve summoned the full number of the disciples and said, 'It is not right that we should give up preaching the word of God to serve tables. Therefore, brothers, pick out from among you seven men of good repute, full of the Spirit and of wisdom, whom we will appoint to this duty. But we will devote ourselves to prayer and to the ministry of the word.'" The church in Jerusalem needed to ensure that food was being distributed to the widows properly. The Twelve suggest that they appoint seven men to this task. God works through the church to call Stephen to this duty. Note that Stephen's public ministry eventually gets him killed.

03
- - - -

GOD DIDN'T CALL
YOUR WIFE AND
YOUR KIDS

God called *you* to plant the church. In every calling in Scripture one things is clear, God is directly and specifically addressing the man. The woman might hear the call, she might support the call, but it was the man's call. I'm not saying that God can't call a woman to church plant (we'll discuss that later), but when God calls a man to do something, his calling does not automatically become his wife's calling. The reason this is important is that church planting can become this dual-calling-ministry-thing that makes things messy. It can work, but just because you can make something work doesn't mean it's right. Again, look at Abraham. Whom did God call? Abraham. Obviously, Sarah was going with him, but her role was that of Ephesians 5 and 1 Peter 3: submission and support.

The bottom line is this: God called you to plant the church and that should set strategic boundaries for the role your wife and your kids will play in church planting. These boundaries might seem like small distinctions, but they can be game-changers. Think about it this way: if a guy has a job at the CIA, he understands that his wife doesn't work at the CIA—and neither do his children. If a guy is an airplane pilot, he is not going to put his wife into the cockpit to fly the plane; she doesn't know what she is doing and she hasn't been trained. He is certainly not going to make his kids the flight attendants. We need to think through what we are doing.

Our tendency is to think that if the guy is called to plant then the whole family is automatically called. So, in our church planting assessments, we ask the wives, "Do you feel called?" This type of inquiry can coerce a woman into feeling she has to be called to plant a church just because her husband is called. Further, this can lead to an exaltation of her supposed calling to plant a church above the other clear callings of God on her life, and that is dangerously wrong. Her calling is to be a helpmate; in addition to that, she may have a calling to be a CEO, a nurse, or a PhD student. Yet, we often effectively say that church planting takes priority over the other callings in a women's life, so that she is expected to sacrifice those things to plant a church she is not even called to plant.

So, if your wife says, "I'm not a big fan of church planting; I'll go along and support you, but I don't want to lead a Bible study," what do you do? A lot of people might say that you shouldn't plant a church, but I disagree. Does the woman have to be as bought in as the man? No. What the woman has to be is obedient to God's will. God's revealed will for the woman is to submit to, love, and support her husband and live out any particular callings that God has given her. Just as she would if her husband was in the CIA or an airplane pilot. Sometimes I think we have lost our minds! Church planting is one of the fields in which where we demand the wife have the same vocation as her husband. We won't let the wife preach—we certainly won't let her do that!—but we demand that she has a similar calling. This can lead to an exaggeration of a wife's role in church planting and a diminishment of her other God-given callings, and I want to protect you from this.

It's the same story with your kids. A man's calling to be a husband and a father is just as valid as his call to be a church planter. If you are a planter, your kids aren't automatically recruited into church planting, and you need to be conscious of that. Someday God might call your children into church planting, but your call is not their call.

If God wants your wife or kids involved in church planting, guess what He'll do? He'll tell them. Some might say, "What about headship of the home?" But God didn't have a problem talking to Samuel when he was a kid just because Samuel's father was the head of the household. He didn't have a problem talking to David when he was a kid. He didn't have a problem talking to Josiah—Josiah was eight years old when he became king. God didn't have a problem talking to John the Baptist in the womb. God can call your wife and your kids to their own callings and as a planter you should be cautious about how much of the church planting burden you place on your family's shoulders.

Does a planter's wife have to be *the* church planting wife? No. Can she just go to church and serve? Yes.

Can a planter's kids just be kids and play with Legos? Yes!

04

YOU SHOULD
NOT PLANT
A CHURCH

"Do not enter the ministry if you can help it," was the deeply sage advice of a divine to one who sought his judgment. If any student in this room could be content to be a newspaper editor, or a grocer, or a farmer or a doctor, or a lawyer, or a senator, or a king, in the name of heaven and earth let him go his way . . .[4]*—Charles Spurgeon*

Do whatever you can to do something else. Church planting is not the greatest thing on the planet—contrary to what some people may believe. That may sound a bit less than spiritual, but it's true. Doing something else (and by doing something else I mean not being a lead church planter) is not doing something less; doing something else is just as dignified as church planting. I don't think God has tiers in the kingdom in which the church planter gets to reside in a much higher place than the greeter at Walmart. All work is dignified as long as it is done to the glory of God. We know this for a fact: if the goal of church planting is actually making disciples—which means that you make new ones and equip existing ones—that can be done as a greeter at Walmart *or* as a fully-funded church planter. And we also know this: *sometimes the greeter at Walmart is more effective at making disciples than the fully funded church planter.* So when I say do something else, it's not to discourage you. It's okay to do something else.

There is more than one way to church plant. Paul planted churches with teams and the team members had different roles. You may not be called to be the lead church planter. You might be called to be in a support role. *In fact, the future of church planting hinges on all the people who are going to do something else. If we don't have a movement of people who do something else, church plant-ing—like all other Christian missional fads—will be just that: a fad. We won't even be talking about it in the next five or ten years, we'll be on to something else.* But if we have a bunch of people who do something else and support church planting, it will be here for generations to come. Said simply, a lot of people who want to be involved in church planting should probably not be full-time lead church planters, they should do something else and support the guy who has a clear call.

We need to expand the ways in which we think about church planting. We act like there is only one way (being the primary church planter) and if that's not you then get out of here. That is not the biblical precedent. Do we have any Lukes in our church planting model? Do we have any Timothys? Are there any Apaphrodituses? Paul had a squad; we need to get back to the squad men-tality. Just because you are passionate about church planting doesn't mean you have to be a lead planter. Do something else—you can still be involved in church planting.

05

ANOINTING

Outside of a calling, anointing is the most important characteristic for a church planter. In simple English, anointing is God's favor. To be anointed means that there is a special presence and favor of God in your life. Special means that it's beyond ordinary; it's beyond common grace.

Anointing is manifested in extraordinary occurrences. Extraordinary is people calling you on the phone out of the blue, saying, "Hey, have you ever thought of going to Baltimore and planting a church? We'd like to plant a church in Baltimore and we want to fly you out there and see if God is calling you to do this." Extraordinary is having a follow up call, saying, "We've been fasting and praying, and we feel like God wants us to bring you on as our missions pastor and send you out to Baltimore to plant a church." Anointing is when all the pieces fall into place and you can't explain them except for this one fact: that the God of the Bible is real. Anointing is what happens when God puts His special favor on someone.

Illustrations? *Abraham.* How do you go into a city, pretend your wife is your sister, and then walk out a millionaire? Because you're anointed. *Joseph.* How do you get trafficked into slavery and end up second-in-command? Anointing. The Scripture repeatedly says that the favor of the Lord was with Joseph (see Genesis 39:21). *Moses.* How do you have a hot temper, murder someone, go away and shepherd sheep for forty years, and then at the age of 80 come back and lead an exodus with millions of people out of the greatest kingdom on earth? Anointing. If you want to know if you've been anointed by God for a task, here is what you should look for: things in your life that can only be explained by God's activity.

You should see unexplainable things in your life when you decide you are going to plant a church—and there should be a lot of them.

Now, the anointing of God doesn't always mean you will have success in accordance with the way we like to keep score. This isn't the Super Bowl or March Madness. Sometimes God anoints you to die. Sometimes God anoints you to be that lonely voice in the wilderness. But, anointing is always effective in God's purposes—always. The cross is the most devastating thing to ever happen on our planet, but it saved billions of souls. It wasn't cool that Joseph was in prison, but because of the anointing on him it became a means to his rule. So, anointing isn't always calculated in the way we like to calculate things. However, when you are anointed you should be able to look around at your life and say, "The only way I can explain all this is that God is real."

If you don't have that anointing you shouldn't plant a church—at least not until you do. You should go and do something else, and God is going to love you and be pleased with you. Ask yourself: what are three extraordinary things that God has done while calling you to plant a church, things that can only be explained by God's existence? If you can't come up with a list quickly, that should give you pause. Anointing is important, and you can't concoct it. It only comes through God's sovereign gifting.

06

THE MOST RELEVANT BOOK IN THE BIBLE FOR CHURCH PLANTERS

Ecclesiastes.

07

YOU'RE NOT GOING TO PLANT A MEGACHURCH

It's true for ninety-nine percent of planters.

Take a look at the stats. According to the Hartford Institute for Religion Research,[3] fifty-nine percent of U.S. Protestant and other Christian churches (excluding Catholic/Orthodox), had 7–99 attendees; thirty-five percent had 100–499 attendees; four percent had 500–999 attendees; and four hundredths of a percent had 2000–9,999 attendees.

You are going to plant a small church.

God is okay with that. The question is: are you? Are we? Think about it. A church is a group of disciples that are gathered around the Word of God and the ordinances of God to do the will of God—that's the *ekklesia*. Scripture doesn't put a numerical threshold on what makes you a church—so why shouldn't we plant small churches? Most of you are going to plant small churches and that's okay. As far as we know, Jesus had only twelve committed disciples (one of them turned out to be a betrayer so really it is more accurate to say eleven) and all of them got shaky when times were rough. We know there were others who followed Jesus at times, but we also know that most people had left Him by the time He made it to the cross.

In addition, to the precedent of Jesus, a brief survey of redemptive history also suggests that we should expect small churches. There was at least one megachurch in Jerusalem, and some people argue that Antioch was a megachurch, but most churches in the first century met in homes. We're not talking about the Malibu zip code, where you can pack two hundred people in one house. If you do an archaeological study of the apostolic era, you will find out that most houses, and that means most churches, were small.[5] Paul, the consummate church planter who planted a lot of churches, planted small churches, and for most of those churches their multiplication was small. So the bottom line is this: small churches are okay.

Most guys are never going to plant a megachurch. Many of them are depressed because of their church size. They—and we—need to repent of this nonsense. The parable in Matthew 25 tells us that God gives some people five talents, some two talents, and others a single talent. *God expects you to be faithful with what He has given you.* If God gives you twenty-five people then your question is how to make disciples of twenty-five people, and what multiplication looks like for me with twenty-five people. What does growth look like for me with twenty-five people? I know that our denominations and church planting movements don't want to hear this, but it's true: most of you are never going to plant a big church, most church planters are never going to plant a big church, and most churches are going to be small. God is okay with that.

But, we are not talking about dead churches, disobedient churches, and churches that refuse to multiply or participate in evangelism and church planting. We're talking about small *churches*.

Additionally, there are things small churches can do that big churches can't. There is a reason why, when the U.S. wanted to kill Osama Bin Laden they didn't send the whole army in there: it wouldn't have worked. They sent a SEAL team— an elite, quick moving team. Small churches and church plants need to recognize their assets and not get stuck staring at big brother down the street who is running five hundred people. Small churches are agile and they can be mobilized quickly. Why don't we take advantage of this? Why don't small plants join other small plants to do big things? Why don't small plants join big churches to do big things? Why don't small plants ask bigger churches to come and help them? Why doesn't the little guy think to himself, "I have a role in this Kingdom thing too?" There is a strategic place for small churches.

As a matter of fact, if we were really godly we would actually target places with small populations for church planting. We're so worried about millions of people going to hell that we don't care about a thousand going to hell. We should care about everyone. We focus on the city of one million people where only fifty thousand of them know Jesus, but we don't mourn over the city of ten thousand where only five hundred know Jesus.

What about a small city church-planting initiative where we mobilize our churches to plant churches in small cities? When are we going to intentionally plant churches that will only have twenty or forty people and are only going to reproduce on a small scale? It's actually cheaper to plant in small cities. It is cheaper to support the planter and it is fiscally way more plausible.

My friend Ronnie Martin, in Ashland, Ohio, has a vision to plant churches in all the small towns in his state. He'll never get any publicity for it. No one will ever ask him to speak at a conference. Our exaggerated focus on big numbers is carnal and demonic. It's glitz and glam. It's calculated diminishment of the small, and that's the devil's tactic. He tells us, "Oh, those people don't matter, go for the big place."

Small churches are arguably more "biblical" than big churches. Similarly, small groups of people are more "biblical" than big ones. Think about it, as a general rule when God wanted to do something big in the past, He used small groups of people. God usually uses small, insignificant groups of people to do big things and a lot of times they never live to see their success. We need to re-alize the dignity, honor, and immense pleasure that God has in a planter plant-ing a church—reaching a handful of people and pastoring them faithfully. God doesn't see that person as any less honorable than the guy who has planted a church that runs twenty thousand, has planted two hundred churches, and has sent out one hundred missionaries. They are both His kids and the blood of Christ cleanses them both from their sin. They both have the imputed righ-teousness of Christ. There are no penthouses in heaven; we will all be together praising the Lamb. One guy by God's grace led twenty thousand to Christ; an-other guy by God's grace led fifteen people to Christ. It was all Christ. God did it all and He receives all the glory. Small churches are glorious—and you will probably plant one.

08
- - - -

DON'T START ANYTHING

A successful church plant is something you join—not something you start. Church planting is about joining God in what He is already doing rather than starting something brand new. God has already given us the great commission, and the Spirit is here to lead and guide us in it. The whole trajectory of human history is headed towards people coming to faith and a great white throne judgment in which those of faith are appointed to eternal life and those who don't believe are sentenced to eternal death. God is already up to something and He has been at work since creation. Multiplication and mission has always been His mandate.

Throughout redemptive history, God has invariably called people to join something He was already doing. God had the idea of having a chosen people, and then He called Abraham to start it. The call to church planting is really just an invitation to join God in what He is already doing. Practically, this means that rather than looking to start something new, you are looking to see where God has already started working. Church planting is more about using your discernment to find out what God is up to and how He wants to use you in His plans, than it is about innovation.

You can see this pattern clearly in the book of Acts. The Macedonian vision is a great example of this. Paul had a vision of a group of people saying come help us and, surprisingly, he concluded that they should go proclaim the gospel there. It was obvious that God was already doing something in Macedonia and that Paul needed to get in on it.

Think about the missional movement of the first publicly constituted church in Acts 1. How did they plant churches? Their mission started because persecution sent them out, and then they found what God was already doing wherever they went. The planting strategy in Acts doesn't appear to be too complex: the apostles simply went where God took them; in a lot of cases, as with Lydia and Cornelius, when they arrived in a new place they found out that God was already working. The existence of such missional priming is only natural, considering that the book of Acts began with the risen Christ telling the apostles that they will be His "witnesses in Jerusalem, and in all Judea and Samaria, and to the ends of the earth" (Acts 1:8). This is the pattern in Acts and in the rest of Scripture: God has something planned and then He draws people into it.

This pattern is also observed in the promises made to Israel. Effectively, God says, "I'm bringing you into a promised land. Houses you didn't build, cisterns you didn't dig, vineyards you can just eat from" (see Deut. 6:10–11). *God is always ahead of you.* He's already working. You don't need to start anything—you need to join God in something He has started.

In addition, there are dangers in thinking that you are "starting" something. First and foremost, there is an incredible temptation to pride. If you started it, you darn sure are going to be the one who finishes it. And if you started it, and not God, then you probably aren't going to be as willing to edit it along the way. Also, if you have the mindset that you are starting a church, whoever you start the plant with is probably going to be infected with that same prideful outlook, and then you develop a core group psychology that is extremely toxic.

In addition, if you started it then the ceiling is *you.* You have a ceiling (every planter does), but if God starts it there is no ceiling. If you are convinced that you started the church then the church can never grow beyond you—whether that be in terms of ideas or number of people. So too, if you started the church, who does the glory go to? You. And that's wrong; God started your church and deserves all the glory for it.

It is harder to start something than it is to join something. This is one of the main reasons planters have so many hardships. They are literally trying to start something out of nothing, and the only person who can do that is God. If there is nothing there … then there is nothing there … and there is nothing you are going to do to make something be there. You're not God. If God is not doing something, you're not going to make something happen. Thats why, once you suspect a call to planting, you need to look for those extraordinary things in your life; you need to confirm that God is up to something already.

Ultimately, starting a church is something spiritual. We know that we can't do anything spiritual. So don't start anything, just figure out what God is already up to and accept His invitation to join it.

09

DON'T UNPACK
YOUR BOOKS

If you're going to plant a church, you've got to be intentional. If you are a guy who is going to want to study and read a lot, you need to think realistically about this. If you are planning on spending the majority of your time as a planter studying and reading, you need to reconsider whether planting is for you In the initial stages of church planting, you should spend most of your time with people. You need to be developing people, cultivating relationships, sowing seeds, and sharing the gospel. It is called church *planting*. If you are going to plant a garden, you don't spend eighty percent of your time reading about it. You go get a shovel, dig, sow the seed and water the ground.

When I was church planting, I unpacked some of my books but not all of them. I didn't want to get trapped in my library; God didn't send me to Baltimore to sit in my office. He sent me to Baltimore to go out and meet people, make disciples, and persuade people to the love of God in Christ Jesus. He sent me to spend time with and develop leaders, to raise support and partners, and to get to know people. I couldn't do that sitting in a coffee shop reading books for four or five hours a day. That's not a bad thing to do, but if you are planting a church—at least in the initial stages—you should be out in the community.

Everywhere we look in the Bible, when somebody is on mission, they are on mission. They spend a lot of time actually in the mission field. Think about this text in Mark 6:30-31

The apostles returned to Jesus and told him all that they had done and taught. And he said to them, "Come away by yourselves to a desolate place and rest a while." For many were coming and going, and they had no leisure even to eat.

When the disciples were on mission with Jesus they spent so much time with people that Jesus sends them away to rest. This plan is actually interrupted because people see them on their way and follow them—the feeding of the five thousand is what ensues.

So here is my suggestion: read all the books you need to read first. Fill your theological, mental, and emotional tank up so that you are full, and then go spend it. View church planting like a road trip. You are not going to stop in the middle of a road trip and spend four or five hours looking at maps. You're not going to stop in the middle of a road trip and spend three hours on Google figuring out what you're going to do when you get there. Typically, you are going to plan that all out beforehand. A road trip is about execution, and church planting is the exact same way.

For a lot of planters, it's hard to figure out why they aren't successful until you start asking them practical questions like, "How much time have you actually spent with people who are not in the church? How much time have you spent developing leaders? How much time have you spent outside of your house?" Most of the men who have been successful in church planting have spent a large part of their time with people. When Jesus came to Earth, the Bible indicates that He spent the majority of His time with people. In the book of Acts, when they went to plant churches, they spent the majority of their time with people.

Here is the reality of it: we should read, but most preaching is not going to get better by reading. Reading is very important, but in your early days as a planter reading is probably not going to be one of the top ways that you will enhance your ministry. The way to become a better church planter is by doing it, observing it, and having a good coach to help you. Reading about church planting is usually only a minor influence.

Reading can end up serving as an escape for planters who aren't really into people and for planters who don't really want to do anything. They figure that when people ask, "What have you been up to?" They can at least answer, "Oh, I've been reading this book." Last time I checked I don't think anyone is cutting you a check for a $1000 a month so that you can read books about church planting. You're not funded to read books—you are funded to reach people. The majority of your time should be spent with people. That's why you are funded, that's what people are praying for, and that's why churches send you.

Don't unpack your books—at least for the first six months. Pick a few commentaries for things you are preaching through, leave the rest of your stuff in boxes, and use the time you'd spend meddling with books to get out there and be with people.

10

IF YOU
CAN'T PREACH

Don't plant.

11

----

10 COMMANDMENTS
OF PREACHING

1. Pray until it hurts—and don't stop.
2. Study like its a final exam .
3. Preach the text.
4. Know yourself and be yourself.
5. Engage the head, move the heart and give their hands something to do.
6. Know your audience.
7. Work on your preaching in order to get better.
8. Keep it moving and keep it short.
9. Get to Jesus.
10. Let the gospel contaminate everything.

12

YOUR PRIMARY
STRATEGY

Prayer is *the* primary strategy for church planting. It should be your pre-eminent strategy for church planting. You should pray always, but especially in church planting and especially in the beginning of the planting process. People might not like that I say "especially in the beginning," but that's the truth.

When you are initially starting the church, you should spend a significant amount of time in prayer for the church plant. How much time? Well, if it's your primary strategy then you should spend a lot of time doing it. If you need a number, start with a minimum of one hour a day. Or start by setting aside one day a week for fasting and prayer and spend three or six hours in prayer that day. Scripture tells us that Jesus once spent a whole night in prayer. Most planters have never spent a whole night in prayer. They've spent a whole night with people, a whole night depressed, a whole night doing a lot of stuff, but they've never spent a whole night in prayer—and they probably should.

We know that God hears and cares, and that church planting is part of His mission. So you should pray confidently, knowing that, as John says, "if we ask anything according to his will, he hears us. And if we know that he hears us—whatever we ask—we know that we have what we asked of him" (1 John 5:14b–15).

Biblically, the priority of prayer is not difficult to demonstrate. The Church—the global, universal Church that Jesus promised He would build—was started with a prayer meeting. Acts 1 tells of the apostles in Jerusalem pre-Pentecost that "All these with one accord were devoting themselves to prayer, together with the women and Mary the mother of Jesus, and his brothers." (Acts 1:14). The church in Philippi started with a prayer meeting. Paul and his crew met Lydia at a prayer gathering, and then a number of baptisms followed her conversion. Cornelius' house was devoted to prayer; in response God sent Peter to proclaim the gospel to Him and a large gathering of people—and many of them, if not all, subsequently believe it. Jesus prayed prior to major decisions and events. The priority of place given to prayer in Scripture should be reflected in your own life and church—prayer should be your primary strategy too.

It's a sad reality that people plant churches without spending a lot of time in prayer. It grieves me when I go to a church and there is not a lot of prayer in the liturgy. The service might be an hour and a half long and only one minute of that is allotted to prayer. That is unacceptable.

I've said this for years, but it's very interesting to me that we can get people to fly across the country to hear a man speak—we can get thousands and sometimes tens of thousands of people to fly across the country to hear music—but if you were to hold a conference and say, "This conference is for praying," no one would come. If you are planting a church in this era, you are planting in a culture that places too little value on prayer, and you need to be cognizant of that.

We all know what prayer is and we all know the incredible promises Scripture makes about it, but we devote so little time to it. Maybe that's why we are so powerless. Maybe that's why God doesn't move. If He did, then we would get all the glory because we are full of activity rather than prayer.

One of the few times I saw a heavy reliance on prayer modeled was in a church I visited over a decade ago. This is how they began their liturgy: the pastor came up and said "Lets begin our worship" and then everyone got on their faces and prayed for half an hour. It was beautiful. You've heard about how prayer meetings in the past have started revivals as well. One of my heroes was Charles Spurgeon. He had a boiler room where hundreds of people prayed for him while he preached. When he was asked why he thought his preaching was so successful and why he had seen so many conversions, he attributed it to all the people he had praying for him.

The message you will get from a lot of church planting organizations is, "Let us equip you, we have everything you need—of course, you should pray, but what's really important is that you get assessed, trained, and coached by us." Those things are important for you to do, but be careful about using them as replacements for prayer. Having prayer as your primary strategy doesn't come naturally—it's something you have to fight for. If you don't have a serious commitment to prayer, then you don't have a serious commitment to plant.

13

DON'T PLANT
BY YOURSELF

You should not plant by yourself. If you are the only one setting out to plant a church, that should cause you to do some serious questioning—not necessarily of your calling—but at least of the timing of your calling. Your providential solitude might be an indication that God wants you to wait to plant a church.

I say this because we don't see any solo planters in Scripture. If the Bible is a sufficient book and we are to learn from it and get our ideas from it, then you are lacking the support of scriptural wisdom in your endeavor to plant on your own. There is no record in the New Testament of a solo planter; everyone was a part of a team. As a matter of fact, every church plant in the New Testament was planted out of a preexisting church. The idea that you'd send one guy out by himself would never have entered the New Testament mind. It would have been insanity—yet we do it all the time today.

You know why we plant churches by ourselves? We're just proud. We're sophisticated, we're modern, we have the internet, jobs, training, mechanisms, smartphones, laptops, and degrees. We trust in all of that instead of the example God provides in Scripture.

In Luke 10, when Jesus sends out the seventy-two, He puts them in pairs, and other gospel passages indicate the same pattern (cf. Mark 6:7). In Acts, you don't see anyone functioning on their own. Everyone is in teams and everyone has support. If we really want to do things like Jesus, even Jesus went out and gathered a group of guys to work alongside Him before He really started rolling in His ministry. *Even Jesus didn't church plant alone.* And you shouldn't either.

Just because you're doing it and it's going okay doesn't mean it's right. God could just be extending mercy to you, and blessing you in spite of your error.

Scripture also tells us that two are better than one. In the beginning—before there was sin—God did say "It is not good that the man should be alone" (Genesis 2:18). So, how could it be good that a guy be alone in church planting? Therefore, if you are the only one setting out to church plant, you should wait until you have a team. And if you've already planted by yourself, you should make assembling a team your top priority. You are going to need a co-laborer, and, if you don't have one you need to go find one. Pray for God to bring you somebody or lead you to somebody. And pray hard. Spend hours in prayer and fasting. Then use means—do whatever you need to do to recruit a co-planter.

Beyond the biblical precedent for team planting, does our psychology even have the capacity to plant a church by ourselves in a healthy way? Were we ever meant to do that? I don't think so. If you plant by yourself, you are bringing a lot of temptation upon yourself. Planting by yourself makes it almost impossible to keep the ten commandments—particularly the second, fourth, and tenth. It is very difficult when you're planting by yourself not to idolize church planting. If you have the desire to plant alone you need to talk to God about that and figure out where that comes from.

Also, think about the struggles that single parents have; as a single church planter you are taking a similar burden on yourself. You gather a bunch of sheep that need to be cared for, and then you're the only one to do it. Most planters aren't gifted enough, mature enough, or attractional enough to pull it off by themselves. When you plant by yourself, guess what is exacerbated? Your weaknesses. You need people to cover your weaknesses and accentuate your strengths, and that only comes through a team.

In an ideal world, you would only plant once you had assembled a full team. We were made to be in community, Scripture is full of "one another" commands, and you are going to need all of the graces that come through others as you work to plant a church. Please don't plant alone.

14

WOMEN SHOULD PLANT CHURCHES (AND THEY MIGHT BE BETTER AT IT THAN MEN)

It is undeniable that women played a major role in church planting in the first century. Women were some of the most committed followers of Jesus during His life. They were in the upper room praying in Acts 1. They were obviously a part of the church in Jerusalem. One of the first church fights, recorded in Acts 6, was sparked by the neglect of widows. Women were part of the overnight prayer gathering for Peter while he was in prison in Acts 12, and when he was freed the servant girl Rhoda failed to answer the door due to her excitement at the sound of his voice—indication that she was quite familiar with the apostle. The conversion of Lydia at the women's prayer meeting in Acts 16 led to the birth of the church in Philippi. Philippians 4 tells us of two other women who played a prominent role in the church in Philippi: Euodia and Syntyche. Paul speaks of these women as "those who have labored side by side" with him in the gospel (Philippians 4:3). Paul's conclusion in Romans 16 is filled with greetings to women who have been a major part of that early church's work. At the very least, Paul names Phoebe, Prisca, Mary, Rufus' mother, and Nereus' sister. Several of the other names listed likely refer to women, but the gender is unclear. Despite what our actions traditionally indicate, there is a preponderance of biblical evidence that women play an essential role in the accomplishment of God's mission.

Expressed positively, here is a doctrinal thesis to guide our thoughts on women and church planting: in God's ecclesial ordering women can do everything but hold the office of pastor or elder. That exception is not an ability thing; that is just an obedience thing. Women could function as pastors, and some women are better preachers and teachers than a lot of men, but God has said that it is not their role. But, that doesn't mean a woman can't plant a church!

What are the elements of starting a church? Sharing the gospel, gathering people, leading people, discipling people, and putting people on mission. A woman can do all those things. And then she can lead the church to prayerfully wait until God sends a man to fill the office of pastor and elder. *A woman can do all of that and God could actually call a women to do that.* Nothing in the Bible restricts her from doing so.

Think about the woman at the well: she met Jesus, got saved, went back into town and told people about Jesus, and then brought others back to meet Jesus (see John 4:1–42). What is that? That is church planting. Can only men do that? No, women can do that too. Women can bring people to Christ, and women can disciple people (see Titus 2). Women can even be involved in the discipleship of men, not just of other women. We have a scriptural example of a women participating in the discipling a pastor and church planter. In Acts 18, Priscilla and Aquila pulled Apollos, a renowned catalytic speaker aside and "explained to him the way of God more accurately" (Acts 18:26c). This married couple—man and woman—both instructed him. Can a women train a man? Yes. Can a women equip a man? Yes. Can a women participate in clarifying a man's calling to planting? Yes. So, women can and should plant churches.

If you are a woman reading this, you need to know that and be open to that possibility. If you are a man, you need to know that women are going to be critical to your church plant—not just to the life of the church, but also to the core elements of church planting. As a church planter, it is important to have at least a couple of women's voices as a part of decision-making. You need to consult them.

I think one of the most difficult people groups for conservative churches to handle is strong, gifted women, and as a result we often fail to utilize their gifts. Rather than doing what we usually do—which is nothing—we should engage them and help them to use their gifts, not being afraid of them getting involved. Focus on what women can do. Can they lead missions trips? Can they sit in on elders meetings and give some advice and counsel? Can they implement decisions that the elders make? They can—and they might be better at doing these things than the men in your congregation.

There is one final biblical wrinkle in this: we know that Timothy learned the faith from his mother and grandmother. Though they didn't know it at the time, they were raising someone who would later be a massive player in the early Christian movement. Spiritual mothering is crucial to church planting. Moms may feel especially excluded from participation in church planting, and assume that there is nothing they can do in this. But they can raise the next generation of church planters—and that is not an insignificant task. Even Jesus, *the* Church planter, underwent the mothering of Mary.

Women have played many important roles in redemptive history; God consistently uses them to do incredible things, and you've got to know that. We need to expand the way we think about women's roles in church planting, and if we do, we'll be better off because of it. Women make up about one third of all seminary students, and that number has been on the rise over the last few decades.[6] What if we had a channel through which some of these women could move into church planting? What if you, as a church planter, went to seminaries looking for women to be catalytic leaders in your plant? Whatever you do, you've got to get women involved in your plant in significant ways.

15

PLANTING VS. PASTORING

You should know the difference.

16

YOU SHOULD
BE THE
MOST GENEROUS
PERSON IN
YOUR CHURCH

Most church planters are going to be the number one givers in their church. This is especially true in the beginning. You should give from day one; even if no one else is giving to the church you need to do so. People should be able to look to you as an example of how to be good stewards of the money God has given them. As a planter and pastor, you can't ask people to do what you are not willing to do. Your church should know you as a generous man. Not because you advertise it, but because it pervades your leadership and people naturally come to awareness of your generosity. Generosity is infectious. If you practice it, there is a good chance your people will catch it and if you don't, they almost certainly won't.

Practically, being generous means you should tithe to God and not tip Him. And you should always be prayerfully considering how you can give more. The Bible says that we should give sacrificially, so one of the questions you need to ask yourself is, how giving is a sacrifice for you? I don't think you've earned the right to be a church planter until you have made a financial sacrifice for the sake of the church.

When a financial issue arises in your church plant, you should be the first to respond—even if that means you have to do it out of your own resources. I knew a planter whose church came up $7,000 short on payroll one month. Some mistakes had been made, and it was the end of the week with payroll due on Monday. So, the planter wrote a check to cover the payroll. He still got paid, but he used his own resources to enable the church to make payroll. That church never had that problem again.

Being a church planter is probably going to cost you—and it should. How invested are you in your church? I don't think you're really invested until it has cost you a lot of your personal money. How much risk do you have in your church plant? Have you mitigated all your financial risk? Are you using everyone else's capital and everyone else's margins so that there is no loss for you?

One of the ways I know a planter is serious is by their giving record. Your giving record should reek of "man, this guy is invested." Money is just one way to be generous, but financial generosity leads to generosity in other areas of your life and in your church plant. And in generosity, God delights. His generosity is beyond our comprehension. God doesn't tithe—He gives everything. He was willing to offer His own Son up to the brutality of the cross for the sake of ungenerous souls. You need to represent that incredible reality to your church.

17

YOU SHOULD
PROBABLY
HAVE A JOB

In the economy of the first century, a very small number of people were wealthy. A huge section of society was poor, and then there was a population of slaves. As a result, it appears that the preponderance of early church pastors functioned bivocationally. In Acts 20 Paul addresses the elders in Ephesus and says that, "You yourselves know that these hands ministered to my necessities and to those who were with me" (Acts 20:34). He then goes on to commend his bivocational status and indicates that he has taught them to do the same.

It's still hard for me to wrap my head around the idea that Paul worked. We know that he didn't work full time—but he at least worked some of the time, and even that is astonishing given all that he did as an apostle and church planter. We know that Paul worked for the sake of the gospel, so as not to bring the gospel under any type of suspicion, as he spells out in 1 Corinthians 9.

The idea that you will get paid as a church planter is not an absolute. The reality is that if we have to fund every single church planter we're not going to plant a lot of churches, because there is just not enough money to fund all the people who want to plant. The need is so great and the resources are so few. But, what you'll find in Scripture is that you don't need a lot of money to plant churches. What you need is God, a gospel, and someone with a calling who is biblically-qualified. If you have that, you can plant churches.

We need to see a resurgence of men—and women—who are planting and who have jobs. I've often said that one of the greatest problems with politics today is that everyone gets paid. The rebuttal to that is "Well, how would they do their job if they aren't full time? How are they going to have their meetings?" My response to that is that it would force them to think about what is actually important. It would make them more effective and force them to be more targeted in their efforts. The same is true of church planters.

We should not take the bivocational example of Paul and others as a hindrance. A lot of full-time church planters don't make it; even though they were given $100,000, they don't always make it to launch. It has been said that you can give the wrong guy a lot of money and it won't work, and you can give the right guy nothing and he will plant a church. History shows that to be true. We need to encourage guys who are working to start to think about how they can plant a church with a job.

I actually think there is a psychological and fiscal advantage to planting a church with a job. If you have a job, you don't have to worry about saying something that causes people to leave the church. If God shows you a direction, you just follow it; you don't have to worry about the two biggest givers in your church leaving if they don't like it. It gives you boldness as a planter if planting is not the source of your money. No matter what you think, if you are collecting a check from networks, denominations, and other people and you are fully dependent on them to support you, *you will have them in your mind when you preach and make decisions about the direction of the church.* Being a fully-funded planter comes with peculiar temptations to please people. In addition, while our economy is on a little bit of a rise, the majority of people are middle-class and under—and that has major implications. In a city like Baltimore, where there are over fifty-six thousand people without a job,[7] you can't expect church growth to correlate with an equivalent increase in finances. So, if you are depending on other peoples money to reach them, that is not necessarily sustainable. What happens when your three or four-year partnership runs out?

You need to think through your income strategy. We've got to reverse the mindset that if you have a job you can't plant and you can't pastor. The majority of the pastors in the book of Acts had jobs or were broke. Think about this: the gospel is spread amongst abject poverty. *The book of Acts is basically broke people peddling a rich gospel.* They didn't have all the money or resources we have, but they catalyzed a movement that has spanned the globe. Like I said, you don't need money to church plant—you need God, the gospel, and people who are qualified to lead.

I've often said that I would take a team of ten nurses to plant a church over and against a team of ten seminary grads. The reason for this is that every nurse is going to come in making $50,000, a cumulative wealth of $500,000, and if everyone tithed off their gross income then the church would start off with an income of $50,000.

We often think that you can't plant if you don't have full-time hours to devote to planting. Don't believe that lie. You need to realize that God can do more in five seconds than you can do in thirty years full-time. God's economy is not like ours. Here is the bottom line: some of you guys should not raise funds to go into full-time ministry. Instead, you should get a good job or keep your job and plant with your job.

18

YOU ARE
YOUR #1
FINANCIAL
PRIORITY

The lead pastor or planter is the number one financial priority in the church. This is because, as a general rule, if the church loses that guy the church is going to face some significant challenges. In many ways, God has made them a keystone of the church. Now, my robust ecclesiology people aren't going to like this because they are going to object that this is all built around the lead pastor. I understand that. I know that the church is much more than the lead pastor and that leadership by a plurality of elders is the biblical precedent, but in most cases the lead pastor is the one most invested in the church—so why should the church not reflect that in how the lead pastor is compensated? Scripture does say that you shouldn't muzzle an ox and that the worker deserves his wages (see 1 Tim. 5:18).

There are few things that annoy me more than cheap churches. I do understand that there are a lot of churches that literally cannot afford to be anything other than cheap. Maybe they are in a poor neighborhood with a poor constituency, or maybe they are in a poor country where the average person earns less than two dollars a day. Those circumstances aside however, it drives me nuts when churches ask their pastors to work full-time and then don't compensate them accordingly. I don't want you to plant a church that is guilty of this. We've already discussed the merits of bivocational planting, and that is God's desire for many people. Those God does call to work full-time at the church shouldn't get ripped off.

I've often said that pastors are going to worry about money or ministry. Churches should pay their pastor enough money, so that where he is not worried about finances and he can give his full focus to ministry. When they do, they should hold him accountable for ministry—I mean really hold him accountable. If he isn't competent or doesn't do his job, they can get rid of him or put him in another place of ministry. High pay should go with high accountability.

Some people are going to ask how much is enough. People always get worked up about making sure pastors aren't getting paid more than a living wage—whatever that means—and that response is just rooted in fear, guilt, and shame. People freak out when a pastor is getting paid $80,000 and don't even blink when a professional athlete signs a $100 million contract with a $30 million signing bonus. We need to get this straight.

Let me give you some rough math on how this could work. If a church knows that their pastor has a sizable family and that housing is going to cost him $1,500 a month—and most financial advisors will tell you that housing should be a third of your budget—then they are looking at a minimum of about $4,500 a month, which adds up to $54,000 a year. In this day and age pastors need to have benefits, which we could roughly estimate at $1,000 a month or another $12,000 annually. If a church does anything with retirement, we are looking at an estimate of around $70,000 for the total package. That figure should change depending on location.

What this means for you as a planter is that you are going to have to lead your people in this. *You are going to have to teach your congregation to pay you a proper salary.* In 1 Timothy, Paul tells Timothy to do just that—and the same goes for you. Part of Timothy guarding what was entrusted to him (1 Tim. 6:20) was teaching the churches that the elders are worthy of double honor, especially those who preach and teach (1 Tim 5:17). Timothy would have been a financial beneficiary of such teaching.

As a planter, if you are going to lead in this you've got to deal with your own fear, shame, and guilt surrounding money. We are careful to not promote a prosperity gospel (with good reason), but we need to make sure we aren't swinging too far in the other direction. The fact is that there are a lot of wealthy people in the Bible. Being wealthy doesn't commend you to God, and neither does being poor—the blood of Jesus commends you to God. God is not opposed to wealth. Adam and Eve were the wealthiest people on the planet. They owned the whole world—all the gold, the onyx, the diamonds, the rivers, the waters, and the animals. It was all theirs and they were supposed to steward it. Some of the greatest biblical characters were wildly wealthy: Abraham, Joseph, Moses, David, Solomon, and others.

A lot of people like to focus on the poverty of Jesus. He was poor for thirty-three years, no doubt. But before and after that? He owns the whole universe. The earth is His and the nations are His inheritance. So God is not opposed to riches.

We need to get over our fear, shame, and guilt with money and stop making the pastorate some kind of monkish calling. Just because you are a pastor or planter doesn't mean you should suffer financially. Most planters worry about money way too much, and that's one of the things that keeps them from being effective. As a planter, if it is possible, you should free yourself from this distraction. Stand up and talk about it. Preach it and exegete it. Christians should be the freest people with money and you need to disciple your people in that freedom.

God has created a world that largely operates on money. People in ministry always say, "It's not about money." But it really is about money. Money is not God and its not everything, but it is a big deal. As a planter and pastor you need to handle it properly. You need to recognize that biblically speaking, you are a financial priority. As best as you are able, put yourself in a financial position where you can put all your focus into ministry. If the church can't pay you, then find a bivocational opportunity or some other source of income. But please don't let your people persist in the disobedience of robbing their pastor of his wages.

19

THE JESUS PRINCIPLE

Jesus never asks anyone to do what He hasn't already done. Replicate this model in your church plant.

20

CHURCHES AND CHURCH PLANTING

Here is what you need to realize as a planter: there are too many men planting churches who don't really come from a church. They may be loosely affiliated with a church, they may be members of a church, but they have not been properly vetted by a church. Planters need to get back to the idea of getting sent by a church. The biblical model is that when you go to plant a church you come from a sending church that has recognized God's calling on your life—meaning that the elders see it and the whole body sees it—and that has laid hands on you and commissioned you to go plant a church. Then, the church that recognizes that calling also resources that calling. Data also indicates that the most effective church planting path is this: actual churches planting and supporting other churches in a direct relationship.[8] As a planter, you need to make sure you have this kind of relationship with your sending church.

Your sending church needs to have an investment in what you are doing. Not all churches have money, so they may need to work with networks, partner churches, and conventions to resource you, but they need to be significantly involved. They can't be just a name on a required line in some paperwork; they need to be actually invested. They need to know where you are going, why you are going, how you are going, and what you are doing. They need to visit you—regularly.

As one pastor said at a conference on this subject, "If you are a true sending church, you give the credit away when the planter is successful, and when the planter falls apart you are the first one on the scene to pick them up." Having that kind of support is going to be crucial for you and you shouldn't try to go out on the field without it.

I'd love to see the day when we wouldn't even need to assess church planters because the local church has already done so. One of the reasons we have so many church planting networks and different ways to assess men is that the local church doesn't always do its job of biblically-vetting church planters. But it really is their job to recognize planters, resource them, and send them. Seminaries can train, networks can give green lights and yellow lights, but the reality is that the local church is the only institution to which God has given the authority to recognize and to send. I'd love to see a resurgence of local churches taking the lead in recognizing, training, and equipping church planters.

As a planter, not only do you need to make sure you have a sending church, but you need to plant your church with the goal of eventually being a sending church. From the beginning, you need to be injecting missional DNA into your church so that they are inclined to go, send, plant, and push the gospel to the ends of the earth. Churches don't become missional by accident and we are all inclined to mission drift. You need to train your church to do the hard work of identifying and assessing people whom God might be calling to plant.

As you are working towards eventually planting a church out of your church, remember this: a lot of churches don't engage in any sort of missionality or church planting because they think they don't have the resources to do so. But you can church plant without "church planting." You don't always have to be the mother or the father or the primary financer of the plant. You can be the cousin, the aunt, or the uncle. In other words, you can help other churches plant churches.

One of the things I would like to see happen is a lot more churches planted by a team where churches come together to plant churches. You see a lot of cooperation between churches in the book of Acts as they worked to plant new churches. The cooperation was predominately around the sharing of ministers, but they also collaborated to deal with famine and the plight of the poor. I'd love to see a revitalization of that model: churches coming together and planting churches together. If your church is strong in administration and finances but weak in evangelism, maybe you can link up with an evangelistically gifted church to do a joint-effort church plant. Churches need to share their giftings and allow others to help them in their weaknesses.

Doing this requires humility and an embracement of big K kingdom over little k kingdom which is something we're not good at. What this means also is that your plant might be able to birth another plant—with the help of others—earlier than you thought you could. Be open to unexpected ways that God might allow you to do things you didn't think you could do so.

The bottom line is this: make sure you are really sent from a church and then prepare your church to send others whenever God graces you with people called to the work—and then don't be afraid to ask for help from other churches to carry out the work God is calling for.

21

THIRTY YEARS FROM TODAY

We've all heard the statistics: more churches close than we plant. I'm going to give you a novel idea: why *don't* we plant churches that will be around in thirty years? When we think about church planting, we often think about the urgency to reach lost people which is not a bad thing. The urgency to see something new started, to gather, go, accumulate, and baptize. But have we ever thought that we want these church plants to be around in thirty years? We are a very "now" generation, and church planting can get wrapped up in the immediacy of missionality. I want you to consider what it would take to plant a church that will be here in thirty years.

You have to view church planting more like a tree than a shrub. Shrubs come up quickly and grow fast, but as a general rule they tap out. Trees, on the other hand, take years to grow. I'm blessed to have some giant trees in my neighborhood; some of them are seventy or eighty feet high and at least that many years old. As you are church planting, you need to have a perspective of longevity.

It's the old idea of the tortoise and the hare. You need to run, not sprint. One of the reasons so many churches don't last is that they make it a mad dash, and everything is happening at an unsustainable pace. You have to deal with pace. I'm not saying to be lazy, but you need to pace the church. If you run your core group into the ground in the first two years, you are not going to be around in thirty years. If your church is go, go, go, and never has breaks and never has true sabbath, then it will almost impossible for you to be around in thirty years. It takes an exceptional leader to have a fast-paced church that doesn't burn out. The reality is that most of us aren't exceptional leaders; we're average leaders and we can't pull it off. Most likely you're going to have a relatively small church, and with seventy or eighty people some things are just going to take a longer amount of time. That should inform your expectations. And if God does bring you thousands, you can always adapt your speed to suit that.

You will also need leaders who are strong and who are different from you in order to be around in thirty years. You need to develop leaders that people can lean into, look to, depend on, learn from, and grow from. If your church plant is all about you, your wife, and your kids doing everything, you're not going to make it. You've got to empower the church to actually be a church. People really do have to be mobilized, and they have to live out the "one anothers." It takes a lot of strain off the leadership when the church functions like it's supposed to, and you are able to get a lot more life out of the church.

Finally, if you are going to be around in thirty years, you need to have the courage to face problems. If you're one of those guys who doesn't like problems, there is a good chance your church isn't going to be around in thirty years. If your church has been around for thirty years, it has faced more problems than you can recall. You have to be a leader who is willing to get into the midst of problems and trust God to deal with it.

You'll also have to deal with unrepentant sin. It's one thing to have people fall in the church and to be merciful, bandage them up, be a hospital to the sick, and be loving. But anyone who has carnal, unrepentant attitudes or behaviors—you'll have to deal with that. You have to confront them and if necessary they need to be removed. You're not going to last if you allow unrepentant sin in the church. The same thing can be said in a thousand other contexts—you're not going to last if you don't face the sin problems in your church. Sin is systemic. It puts down roots and expands. If you allow problems to go unchecked in your church, they will eventually overtake you.

This all comes down to mindset. You need to be able to see beyond yourself. You've got to ask yourself hard questions. If you're not planning to be the pastor for the next thirty years, what do you need to be doing to prepare your church for that? Or, like I said in the preface, plant backwards. Envision your church in thirty years and then work back to launch. It's crucial to think through some of these things ahead of time, rather than just reacting when it's too late.

22

FAILURE

Failure is a reality for all human beings. There is nowhere on the planet where you are going to escape failure. There is no time in your life when you will escape failure. Failure is here because the Fall is real. Ever since the Fall, failure has been a reality. *Everything fails.* Scientists tell us that the sun is some day going to fail us. Technology fails us. Our minds fail us. Our services fail us. Not only do things fail, but people fail. Our pastors, friends, wives, and kids all fail. It's just a reality. Since that is true, you should expect failure in church planting. You should expect failure to be a regular part of your vocation as a church planter.

Failure is surrounded by three primary emotions: shame, fear, and guilt. The first failure in human history is recorded in Genesis 3, and shame, fear, and guilt can all be observed in Adam and Eve's response. Since then, shame, fear, and guilt are the emotions that dominate our experience prior to our failure, during our failure, and after our failure.

It is incumbent upon you as a church planter to have a biblical view of failure, steeped in truth about who God is and what He has done in the gospel. The reason that is so important is that everybody on the planet has their own remedy for failure. It may be pleasure, avoidance, social media, ice cream, movies, sports, or depression, but everyone has one. Christians have been given a canon—a whole book—about how God solves human and systemic failure in the gospel. The Bible is one giant book of failure, and God is in the mix reversing it all. You need to be familiar with that.

The two most helpful things for processing failure are the person of God and what He has done. Or simply, God and the gospel. Understanding who God is and understanding what He has done in Christ are the greatest remedies for dealing with failure.

The reality of planting is that you are going to fail—everything is not going to go well. You're going to have some major setbacks. There has never been a person post-resurrection who started a church that hasn't had to deal with failure. Every man in every age that has ever tried to do something has suffered failure. Paul had Demas forsake him (2 Timothy 4).

There are different types of failure. With planting, you are dealing with a failure of plans—plans to see a church planted. These plans get thwarted. People quit coming, people don't give, people give you a hard time, and people criticize your family. You need to have a gospel-centered way to perceive, process, and deal with failure.

Church planting, whether you like it or not, is a lot like starting a business. And statistics say that most businesses fail. Church planting is much the same. You're almost always starting with very little and trying to do something great. It's not like cities are all giving us the Macedonian call, begging us to come help them. Our networks and denominations aren't having their doors beat down by mayors asking for church plants. It's not like the president is putting in the annual review, "We need church plants." The flesh abhors the cross and church planting. You are going up against a lot. So failure should be an acceptable reality. It's like NASA going to Mars—they know the majority of things they try, at least initially, are going to fail. Jordan missed more shots than he made. Steve Jobs was a great innovator, but he went through a lot of failure.

Few things will cause you to question your call and move you to quit faster than failure. Most planters quit because of failure. They try to the best of their ability, but at some point their failures overcome them. They're preaching a Bible that is full of God using failures, but they begin to let their failures in church planting become their identity. The psychology of the flesh says, "If I am failing at church planting then, I am a failure." But failure is not final—*Jesus' blood is.* We believe a gospel that says that there is no condemnation for those of us in Christ Jesus and that His righteousness has been imputed to us, so that in the sight of God we are not failures—we are His children. God knows that the spirit is willing and the flesh is weak, so He has made provision for our failures.

Planters are typically more accepting of other people's failures than their own. And they're typically more accepting of failure from a soteriological point of view than a practical view. So they accept that they fail in terms of their relationship with God, but don't extend that same theology to their practical failures—which is a tragedy. Now, I'm by no means saying that the guy who has been out in the field for five years, has seen no salvations, can't preach, and doesn't really want to be in the ministry, should just overlook failure and bounce ahead. There is a time for quitting, but most guys are going to feel like quitting when they need to persevere. And to planters who are presently struggling with failure, I want to say this to you:

1. God does love you. He does. And he does not love you less because you have failed at church planting.
2. You are not your failure. You are a man made in God's image, redeemed by Jesus' righteous life and wrath-bearing death, and Christ's blood is pleading for you.
3. God can use your failures. And He probably will use your failures in planting more than He will use your successes. Jay-Z, one of the most acclaimed rappers of all time, has said that he learned more from his failures than his successes. Your failures usually cause you to go inward and ask questions. When you succeed you don't tend to ask why that was successful. You tend to become what Tonic from the Cross Movement called an "accolade thief."[9] When we succeed we take credit for it. When we fail, it's a great opportunity because we ask why.

   I think one of the reasons God allows failure in our lives as planters is because He is after our Christlike conformity. He is after manifesting his love and care for us, and sometimes the only way we will see it is through failure. Romans 8:28 is true for church planters. too: "We know that in all things God works for the good of those who love him." (Romans 8:28a). Even your failure.
4. God uses people whom the world would classify as failures. With few exceptions, most of the men God used in the Bible had major failures in their lives.
5. This is why you need a real sending church. When you fail you are going to need some people who can really help, really be patient, and really be like God to you. In the event that your church planting venture does not work out, you're going to need a church to help you through the recovery process.

Memo to existing churches: everybody wants to send out the guy who knocks it out of the park, so that we can all "praise God." Or, more honestly, so that we can look good. The reality is that you are probably going to send out guys who are going to fail, and you need to be humble enough to go get them and restore them, because God might be calling them to something else. But don't be discouraged; you're better off being the church that tries to plant ten times and fails than the one that never tries at all. God will honor your faith and hope as you pursue His will in the world.

I'm going to conclude with a personal reflection on failure that has been meaningful to me:

> *To succeed you must be fearless,*
> *relentless, courageous, and focused on*
> *obtaining the objective, and at the same time*
> *impervious to hostility and failure.*

23

YOU ARE
NOT AN
ISLAND

Church planting is not an ecclesiological island. Get to know and work with other churches in your region (even if they aren't in your denomination).

24

DON'T FIGHT
TO KEEP
PEOPLE

You can't want something for someone more than they want it for themselves. The people who God wants you to have at your church will want to be there. One of my good friends told me how, after preaching, someone came to him and said, "You know, you preach like we are never going to come back." He was so anxious about people potentially leaving that it was affecting the way he delivered his sermons.

Of course, we all want to grow and we all want to keep people, but the reality is that our mission is not to grow—it's to make disciples. In today's world, especially if you are planting in the West, there are a lot of good churches people can choose from, and where they attend will probably boil down to personal preference. So don't waste your time trying to convince people to either join you or stay with you—especially when there are thousands and millions of people around you who don't know Jesus, but might want to be with you if they only knew Him.

This is an issue of priority. Spend time with the people who want to be with you and who invest in your church. Don't spend all your time meeting with people who don't want to join you or stay with you. Think about this: when you plant your church, who are you trying to reach? Are you trying to reach people who are coming in and testing you out, trying to find a church? Or are you trying to reach people who don't go to church and don't know Jesus? Inevitably a new church tends to attract people who are already churched and are looking for a new church, but my advice is that you don't spend too much time trying to keep people, especially these people. Focus on reaching lost people.

The Lord showed me years ago that there are some things you just don't want to hold on to, because they will hurt you. If God is trying to take something from you, you need to recognize that and let it go. It might be a blessing. Job did say, "The Lord gave, and the Lord has taken away; blessed be the name of the Lord." (Job 1:21). Let God give you people—and let God take people away from you. Don't be that greedy planter who is paranoid about keeping everybody God gives them. Some people God wants to give you for only a limited time. Some people He wants to take from you. Don't fight to keep people.

25

16-8-4

In my twenty-five years of ministry I have not found a more practical and useful tool for church planting than 16-8-4. This tool can help you specify where you should focus your church planting efforts. You may know that God has called you to plant in a certain city, but not know where in that city you should plant; 16-8-4 will help you answer that.

I was first introduced to 16-8-4 by Barry Whitworth, the state director of missions in Pennsylvania, who developed these metrics to help his state missions staff identify where they should focus their church planting efforts. They were tasked with analyzing sixteen communities, choosing eight of these communities to engage with the gospel, and then selecting four of these communities to establish a church in. I love this system on the state and regional level, but it is incredibly useful for church planters as well.

For you as a church planter, the ratio is going to be more like 4-2-1: you analyze four communities, engage two of them with the gospel, and then determine the one place where you will plant your church. It's very popular for planters to have done some demographic searches and to have gathered some data on the area they intend to plant in. But 16-8-4 has something much more comprehensive in mind.

The first stage of 16-8-4, the analysis, is much more than a few internet searches—it is a full-fledged investigation. You need to be like one of the spies in Numbers 12–14 that God sends into the land to look, to see, and to taste. You need to understand all the details that make up each of the areas that you are analyzing. You need to figure out where people live, why they live there, where they work, what they do for fun, what they think of church, what's happening with other churches in the area, and more. This should all be written down and organized into a report. Once you've done this, you can then narrow your focus to the areas that you believe are best suited to engagement with the gospel.

The next step is to engage your selected locales with the gospel. Because you have done your research on these communities your engagement is going to be much more effective. You are going to have an idea of what might work and what the people might be open to. Whatever open doors to the gospel you found during your study, you should use to determine how you are going to engage the community with the gospel. This could be done through sports leagues, community gardens, coffee shops, parks, universities, door-to-door evangelism— I don't know what it will be for you—but you will have some ideas of what to pursue after your analysis.

And finally, out of your evangelistic engagement, it is likely that a church will be birthed. One of the best things about 16-8-4 is that it allows you to see where God is already at work. Like I've already said, we don't start anything (Chapter 8), we just join God in what He is already doing. Because you've analyzed on a large scope, and then engaged multiple areas, you can proceed with confidence that this is the area where God is already at work and that you should pursue the establishment of a church here.

I don't believe anyone should plant without doing an analysis of the area they are planting in. When Paul went to Athens, he "saw that the city was full of idols" and his observations informed how he engaged the Athenians (Acts 17:16). Notice what he says in his speech to them: "I perceive that in every way you are religious. For as I passed along and observed the objects of your worship I found also an altar with this inscription, 'To the unknown god.' What therefore you worship as unknown, this I proclaim to you" (Acts 17:22b–23). The apostle took time to read the inscriptions on the altars. You also ought to learn the details of your ministry context and let them inform your gospel proclamation.

Another advantage of 16-8-4 is that once you are done with your analytical report you have something in writing that you can use with your core group, new members, and potential partners. It gives you something to send to people so that they can see the specifics of your engagement and its context. I highly encourage you to implement the strategy of 16-8-4 in your planting preparation. Please contact me (see Chapter 46) if you would like further guidance on this.

26

BUILDINGS

In North America, buildings are more important than most of us would like to believe. *Buildings are the most contextual way to communicate the gospel on a consistent basis over the long haul in North America.* Moreover, most planters need a facility to be successful at planting their church. There are a handful of planters who could grow a church in a public dump because they are so anointed, so publicly gifted, and have the ability to amass a crowd anywhere. But most planters need the help of a facility to make disciples, gather disciples, equip disciples, and send disciples out.

Besides that, in the context of North America, when most people think of going to church they think of going to an actual building. When people want to go to the movies they don't typically go to the beach, they don't typically go to the market—they go to the cinema. When people are sick, they don't go to the gym or the school—they go to the hospital. So, it's logical for most people in our culture, when they want to go to church, to think of going to a building. Thats not an inherently wicked thought.

Now theologically we know that the Church isn't the building, but practically people catch more of what they see than what they hear, and people are conditioned by the dozens of church buildings they pass on a regular basis. Plus, they observe us habitually going to the church building. Now, theologically and methodologically we should be the Church outside of the four walls of the building. I certainly believe in the "scattered Monday to Saturday and gathered on Sunday" church. The scattered church is vibrant and active and lives out the "one anothers." But the reality is that the scattered have to gather somewhere.

There has almost been an overreaction against facilities. As a planter, you need to make finding a facility your number one priority—after prayer and making disciples. I'm taking it for granted that you are going to do those two things. And when you do, you're going to need a place to gather people. You can start in a home, but you're not going to end there. I know we're scared of facilities, I know facilities cost a lot of money, I know all the challenges of facilities, but you've got to get one. It needs to be a huge priority for you.

When you get to the place where God has called you to plant, you should devote ten hours a week to finding a facility. If that doesn't cut it after a few months, up it to twenty hours. Make it a priority. Look at every facility, knock on every door, make every phone call, send every email, and get the word out. Meet with principals, business owners, the mayor, or whoever you can that might be able to connect you to a building. Meet with your local denominational organization, local ministries, and other churches. Let everyone know, "I'M LOOKING FOR A FACILITY." That way, when a facility opens up, your name is at the top of the list. Keep reminding people through emails, texts, and calls to "Continue to pray for me as I'm looking for a facility." When a facility opens up, you need to be on the forefront of peoples minds. It's not unspiritual to pursue a facility so vigorously.

God started human history with two people in a geographical location called "Eden." It was a place. After man was banished from the garden, Abraham founds a people, they are taken to Egypt, and then Moses goes and tells Pharaoh, "Let my people go so that they can go and worship." Moses was asking to be let go—to a place. The culmination of that process was David building an actual temple. If places aren't important, why a temple? Why did the *Shekinah* glory go there, why the high priest, the holy of holies, and all the ceremonies? Why would God dedicate so much of the Old Testament to a building if buildings don't matter? Buildings do matter. They're not everything—but they do matter.

In Acts 19, we are told that Paul used the lecture hall of Tyrannus for two years. We don't know if he rented, but we know that Paul had some sort of arrangement that allowed him to use this facility daily. The church in Jerusalem appears to have met in the temple court somewhere (in addition to meeting in houses). God is not anti-facility. It does appear that the New Testament church worshipped predominantly in homes—because that was their economic context. But North America is not first-century Palestine under Roman rule. Most North Americans aren't comfortable coming into your house if they don't know you. They would prefer to talk to you about religion in a public space and that is an okay desire to accommodate.

It's a tragedy that many of our denominations have more churches dying than they do starting. I want to make a plea here: what would it look like for our dying churches to consider turning their properties over to churches that want to live and churches that want to be born? What would it look like to have an inventory of church buildings available for use? What would it look like to actually have a person in charge of coordinating facility acquisition and usage? I actually believe that in every place in North America with high population density, there should be one person whose sole job is to know every potential facility for a church planter.

As a planter, you should be willing to meet anywhere—especially places that are free—as long as it is conducive to the spread of the gospel. You should be in tune with what you think God is calling you to, who God is calling you to reach, and the implications that those two things have for the type of facility you need. Also, be flexible and open to what God brings your way. You may need to alter a facility to meet your needs or you may need to use a facility for short-term purposes. Buildings are important, and especially if you are in North America, you need to have one.

27

THIS METRIC MAY BE AS IMPORTANT AS BAPTISMS

Are you seeing marriages in your plant?

28

THEOLOGY MATTERS

In a sense, all of life is theology lived out. Every philosophy is a child of theology. Every methodology is a child of theology. Theology impacts everything and theology is relevant to everything. Even the atheist's theology—that there is no such thing as God—shapes the way they think and act. Inaccurate or truncated theology tends to give birth to error and dysfunction. As a planter, you can't neglect theology. *You should start your church with a theological creed, confession, or statement that you understand, embrace, and are able to teach.* Don't start your church in a theological vacuum. Start your church on the foundation of a robust theology—because it matters. You will probably want to require your leaders to submit to that same creed, confession, or statement. You can have a more general statement for your congregation, but it is crucial that you and your leaders are united doctrinally. Remember, different theology tends to lead to different practice.

The Bible is a library of sixty-six books that basically bleeds theology. Every page is theology. Theology matters to God and it needs to matter to you, too. If you don't have a good grasp on your theology when you plant, things are going to be a lot more difficult for you. Inevitably, you are going to be asked theological questions and you need to be prepared to give theological answers. You don't want to be working out your answers to difficult questions when you are under the gun. With that said, it's important to remember that we never fully arrive in our theology. Your theology should always be in the process of refinement. I trust that every real Christian, when they read the Bible, grows in the knowledge of our Savior Jesus Christ. Following Jesus is a continual journey of theological disruption and transformation.

We must remember as we plant churches that if we are really reaching the unchurched and lost people, they have a non-Christian theology that doesn't all change at conversion. That's why you disciple them. Jesus told us to make disciples "teaching them to observe all that I commanded you" (Matthew 28:19 NASB). That necessitates theological instruction. When you preach, there needs to be theology in your messages. When you lead communion and baptism, you need to explain the theology of those practices. Your people are going to learn theology one way or another. I believe it is primarily the local church's responsibility to teach them theology—not a website or podcast. And within the local church, the primary onus for theological instruction is on the lead planter or pastor—you. Don't neglect that duty.

29

MY PLANTING PARADIGM

Like most planters, the question I was most often asked while preparing to plant was, "What is your strategy for planting a church in Baltimore?" That question forced me to think deeply about how I was going to pursue planting a church. As I thought about redemptive history, particularly the gospels and the life of Jesus, I came up with the following planting paradigm. Your paradigm won't be exactly the same, but mine is offered here to you as a suggestion.

Planting yourself means that you, first and foremost, establish yourself in the community you are planting in. You get to know your community. You do the homework and spend the time analyzing your community. You build relationships. You get to know the owners of stores. You develop patterns and habits so that people see you regularly. You pray for your community and you learn your community. You learn where the grocery stores are and you begin to get to know the rhythms, patterns, and issues of your neighborhood. You'll know that you have planted yourself when you begin to look like the people you are trying to reach and the place where you are. You'll know you've planted yourself when you begin to earn some credibility amongst indigenous people and indigenous leadership. Planting yourself is all about belonging. You've got to get to the point where you don't feel like an alien or stranger. Again, getting to the point where this foreign place becomes your place. Planting yourself in a city can be illustrated by moving into a new apartment. What do you do when you move in? You bring in your stuff, decorate it in your style, and arrange it your way. Eventually, the place becomes yours. Thats the imagery I have when I think about planting yourself.

Next, you plant your family. Why do you plant your family? Because the Bible indicates that your top two priorities are God and your family. When you go to plant your church, you need to reflect those priorities because if you don't, you will turn planting into an idol; you will put church planting above your love for God and His commands to care for and prioritize your family. So, you plant your family second. You help your wife find new doctors, you help your kids get into the schools, you help your kids make new friends, you have people over, and you become hospitable. You take drives so that you all can get to know the city, love the city, and pray over the city. You just familiarize yourselves with things. You get to the point that your wife is comfortable. I've had a number of planters complain to me that their core group, which is not from the community where they are planting, won't go out and engage the community. I usually respond, "Do the women in the core group know where the post office is?" And when they say no, I usually say, "How do you expect them to engage people when they don't know basic things about the community?" They have to get to a place where they have a sense of belonging.

Obviously, many of the things I mentioned above in regards to planting yourself can and should be done simultaneously. My recommendation is that when you first move to your community, you do most things with your family. You go to a block party—take your family. You go out—take your family. Involve them in the process. Planting your family means actually spending time with your family. As I said before, this new vocation as church planter doesn't mean you get to truncate your vocation as a husband and father—you need to devote time to them. If possible, planting your family also means that you should bring your relatives in to visit you in your new location.

As you plant yourself and your family, share the gospel. Share everything about the gospel. Not just the Four Spiritual Laws or that Jesus died on the cross, but all the implications of the gospel. Share the whole gospel. Share all its benefits. Speak of eternal salvation and the relational, social, and economic dimensions of the gospel. Share the gospel with people. Explore what it means for everything you do to be gospel-centered. When we first started our church, we realized how much we needed clarity about the gospel and how prone we were to drift from the gospel in our core group and in our own souls. Plant the gospel like you are planting a tree—plant it in the front yard so that it's in the forefront, and over time it is going to grow big. You just plant the gospel and you build around it. You don't build the gospel around the church—you build the church around the gospel. You've got to be sharing your faith with people who don't know Christ and with people who do know Christ. Plant the gospel and then invite people to join you in developing in and around the gospel.

You'll notice that I haven't said anything about planting a church yet because that is a result of doing these other things. If you plant yourself, your family, and the gospel you will quite naturally get around to planting a church. But you've planted in accordance with biblical priorities. When you plant yourself, your family, and the gospel before you plant the church, what you've done is model for your people how to live in their context. If you plant this way, you will never call your people to do something you haven't done. You'll just invite them to come follow you, which is discipleship. It will be very natural for you to tell your people to do certain things or to try certain things because they'll see you doing them. Inevitably, as you invite others to join you in following Jesus, you will plant a church. You will establish a group of people who are learning about Jesus together, who are on a journey towards Christlikeness, and have a common objective to go out and share their faith and their lives with others.

Finally, recognize that planting yourself, your family, the gospel, and your church was all done by God. God did it all. As Romans 11 says, "From him and through him and to him are all things." God did it all. Not you. Be very careful at the beginning of planting and the end—if there is such a thing—to give God all the credit and all the glory. If God does allow you to plant yourself, your family, the gospel, and a church, remember that the ability to do all those things came from Him alone.

Every planter has a paradigm. Every planter has ideas of how they're going to go about starting their church. Thus, it would behoove you to spend some extended time thinking about your planting paradigm. Write it out. Share it with a coach, some friends, and some pastors; make sure it is consistent with your theology, philosophy, and methodology; and make sure it reflects the priorities of the Bible. A planting paradigm that directly contradicts 1 Timothy 3 is a stupid paradigm. A paradigm that nowhere reflects loving God with all your heart, mind, and strength, and loving your neighbor as yourself, is not a good one. Take some time to think about your strategies, submit them to the critique of Scripture, and sketch out your own planting paradigm.

30

GET SOME
REAL COACHING

You need to have a coach—and not just any coach, but a competent coach. There are lots of people running around who call themselves coaches, but they're not. All they are is good listeners. They've got big ears and they listen and they make you feel good. *But a coach's job is not to make you feel good, it's to make you effective.* If you want to feel good, go to a counselor or pound some ice cream. A coach's job is to help you become an effective church planter. So it is important that you have a coach who has actually planted a church, and it's important that this person was somewhat successful in their endeavor. If the guy spent a couple of years planting and it never was successful, how can he help you from his experience?

Your coach should also understand your situation. If my church is at the two hundred barrier, how can I speak to someone asking questions about breaking the two thousand barrier? If I planted in the urban inner city amongst African Americans, how can I speak to a guy planting amongst white suburbanites? Of course, there are some transcendent principles in all these situations, but the specific, contextualized applications that we implement are where we live or die. So, you've got to have a competent coach.

You've also got to have a courageous coach. Think of this as if you were going to go into SEAL training. They're not there to make you feel good, they are there to make you an incredibly competent fighter in all disciplines. It's important that your coach has the courage to confront you, challenge you, give you suggestions, make you think about things, and not just rubber-stamp all your ideas.

One of the most frustrating things I see in many coaching relationship is a lack of strategy. It's shocking to me that guys can have one, two, even five meetings with a coach and they still don't have to-do lists, action items, or goals. Progress is important and it doesn't happen by accident. If you spend a year with a coach, here are the fundamental questions you need to evaluate at the end of the year:

1. Are you a better Christian?
2. Are you a better husband?
3. Are you a better father?
4. Are you a better planter?

If the answer to those questions is no, you need a different coach. A real coach will be holistic. A real coach will help you become a better Christian, a better husband, a better father, and a better planter—in that order. Everybody in those four areas of your life should be able to testify to the impact your coach is having on you. It should be that plain. If not, get another coach.

Also, preferably, you need a coach who is is older than you. I'd recommend that you get a coach who is ten or twenty years older than you. They are going to have gone through more life stages, more experiences, and they're not going to be so enamored with you that they are blinded by your successes. Their experience will keep them from overreacting to both your successes and failures.

Finally, consider the character of the coach. Another one of the marks of a real coach is that they are always working on themselves and developing. If you never hear about your coach's own development, then that is not a good sign. Consider affinity as well. There are some guys you are just going to get along with better, and that's not a bad thing as long as they have all the other necessary traits. You need to find a good relational match.

You and your coach need to meet regularly—once a month at a minimum. The best coaching is the kind where you can call at any time. When you're planting a church, things don't always fall into place. Sometimes you can't wait twenty-five days to talk about something. It's important that you get a coach who is available. Having said that, don't expect your coach to give you three or four hours a week.

You should pay for your coaching. Here are two reasons why. First, if your coaching expenses come out of your pocket, you are more likely to actually listen and do what they say. Second, if you're paying for your coaching, you can hold your coach accountable.

If you're paying your coach and they are flaking on you or it's not working, then you can just fire them and get another coach. If you're looking for a good coach, ask planters who have planted, have been successful, and whom you might like to model your planting style after for the names of those who coached them. You're not going to progress as a planter without some real coaching.

31

KEEP THESE
TWO THINGS CLEAR

1. Salvation is free
2. Discipleship costs you everything

32

SIX THINGS MATTHEW 28:16-20 SAYS ABOUT CHURCH PLANTING

1. There will be doubt during it—those who originally heard this doubted.
2. There is a need for authority to do it—the world's systems and its inhabitants are strong.
3. There should be movement in it—go.
4. There is a target or goal to it—making disciples.
5. There should be two things consistently going on in your church—baptisms and teaching obedience.
6. There will always be at least one person involved in making disciples—Jesus.

33

VIOLENCE
AND VOLATILITY

Don't go into church planting unless God tells you to. Planting is a violent and volatile vocation. If you want to know what planting is like, go to your nearest Six Flags Amusement Park and get on the scariest rollercoaster.

That's it.

Except it doesn't last a minute, it's pretty perpetual. This is why I've been saying over and over again: don't plant unless you're called. Even called people will struggle with the volatility of planting. Usually when we talk about volatility, we are talking about the markets. Stocks have volatility ratings. A highly volatile stock has a higher propensity to fluctuate. Planting is just like that: high volatility. Anything can happen...and probably will. The worst case scenarios will happen. Its not, "I wonder if _____ ?" Disasters are going to happen and we know they are going to happen because Jesus invites us into His ministry. A lot of what He went through, you're going to go through. You're going to have a Judas, you are going to have disciples fighting and arguing over who is the greatest, you are going to have doubt, you are going to have people make promises that they don't keep. People will say, just like Peter, "I will never forsake you," and then immediately go out and deny you. You are going to experience abandonment and you are going to have people who hate you and would rather see you dead.

Every new attendee at your church is bringing their own volatility with them. Making disciples is not a stable task. The ministry is crazy. One minute you might be on the shore with Jesus feeding thousands of people, feeling like you are on the mountaintop and the kingdom of heaven is about to be ushered in, and then the next minute you're on a boat in a storm crying out, "Lord, save me!" The ministry is like the weather. Not Cali or Florida weather, but East Coast weather, often unpredictable. One day may be in the 80s and the next day is in the 50s. Just when you think everything is going smoothly, the sovereign God may suddenly swoop in and mix everything up.

If you are planting God is going to give a lot and He is going to take a lot. Things are simply unpredictable, and no matter what system or strategy you come up with, and no matter how hard you pray, there is nothing you are ever going to do that is going to remove the volatility from church planting. No one has ever successfully removed the volatility from church planting. There are a lot of authors, coaches, and others out there who will tell you, "If you do A, B, C, and D, then you'll get E, F, G, and H." It just doesn't work that way. Systems and strategies are helpful, but they aren't going to remove the volatility from planting. So, if you are one of those guys who likes everything perfectly laid out, and you need to know where you are going to be in three years, and you don't like surprises, just do everyone a favor and don't plant. If that is the case, this is the wrong career, vocation, opportunity, and calling for you. Don't go into it.

A lot of planters are jacked up because they are trying to make planting something it will never be. It will never be the nine to five. It will never be the swing shift. It will never be a clock-in and clock-out job. I'm wholeheartedly supportive of regular sabbaths, rest, and keeping the fourth commandment, but planting is just volatile.

The volatility is not only bad; it's good, too. It was Paul who said in 1 Corinthians 16:8–9, "But I will stay in Ephesus until Pentecost, for a wide door for effective work has opened to me, and there are many adversaries." Sometimes things shift in a positive direction and a wide door opens up for you. Sometimes the thing you planted your church for actually starts happening, i.e., people coming and getting saved. Sometimes people get saved in massive numbers. These are all glorious fluctuations and you endure the downswings for the sake of these upswings.

Most of us in the West don't face a lot of persecution, but the reality is this: planting is violent *emotionally, spiritually, psychologically,* and *physically.*

Church planting is emotionally violent. You're just going to get hurt and there is no way around it. And you're going to get hurt a lot. You're going to make bad decisions. Other people are going to make bad decisions. You're going to sin and other people are going to sin. You're going to see people do things that maybe you thought people would never do—and could never do.

Church planting is spiritually violent. I was just sitting with a planter who recounted to me stories of people in his church who had just been baptized and were almost immediately hit with spiritual attacks from the devil. It was crazy stuff. We know we have an enemy who is lurking about like a lion seeking people to devour. There is a war going on behind the scenes. It's a war. Its not a competitive game with referees, yellow and red cards, penalty boxes, flagrant fouls, and commissioner reviews. The devil, if we give him room in our hearts, can drag us right away from the faith.

Church planting is psychologically violent. It wages war with your mind. It's not your white sandy beach with crystal waters and one-or two-foot waves. It's more like the open ocean with twenty- or forty-foot waves and the rogue waves of sixty or ninety feet that just come out of nowhere. Psychologically, you can get really damaged by church planting. Talk to any planter who has been on the field for a few years and they will tell you how planting messes with your mind. One day you will feel like things are great and the next day you will be sure planting wasn't God's calling for you.

Church planting is physically violent. It's violent on your body. You body is the thing that has to process all the violence and volatility we are talking about. Your body houses your soul, and the two are intimately connected. Working late, spending twenty or thirty hours sitting at a desk preparing sermons, doing the setup and teardown for events, logging extended visiting hours with people at coffee shops and in homes, long periods of standing and speaking—all these things have an impact on the body. Planting asks a lot of your body.

Perhaps in no area is planting more violent than when people turn on you, forsake you, leave you, and try to hurt you. The ministry is often most violent when a pastor falls. There is no excuse for the damage we cause as pastors when we fall. But there is a reason why David, when he was given options for the penalty for his sin, chose to fall into the hands of God rather than the hands of men. People can be brutal. We live in a day and age that when you plant a church, and you do something wrong, it can go viral. You are a sinner, so you are going to make mistakes. Public mistakes. It will hopefully not be the kind of dramatic debauchery we imagine when we think of pastoral failures, but you are going to err and your errors are going to be exposed. You are going to be a social media post. It is not if, it is when. Your wife will see it, your kids will see it, and everyone who knows you will see it. Just be forewarned, this is not for the faint of heart.

While I was developing this chapter, my wife chimed in, "Why are we doing this again?" Planting is violent and volatile. If you don't already, you are soon going to know this experientially, not just theoretically—and so is your family. There are going to be times when you think that it's not worth it. But God's grace will abound. The crucifixion of Christ was the most violent and volatile event in human history, and Christ's death was followed by His resurrection. Be prepared to walk through this same pattern of death and life.

34

TWO THINGS
THAT ARE GOING
TO RUIN YOU

There are two things that are going to ruin you in planting your church: the things that you are ignorant of and the things you are unwilling to change about yourself. Those two things (ignorance and unwillingness) will show up in almost every issue you have in planting. In light of this, you need to adopt self-awareness as a mindset.

Your pursuit of self-awareness should not be an auxiliary strategy; it should be central to your efforts to develop as a planter. It is an absolute necessity that you develop an awareness of who you are and how you tend to think, act, and communicate. Romans 12:3 warns, "not to think of [your]self more highly than [you] ought to think." Why would Paul have to tell people that? Because we are sinners and when we fell in sin, our psychologies fell too.

As a planter, you are are constantly operating with your own fallen psychology. It is not going to be natural for you to think rightly about yourself. The best definition of sin I have ever heard is that sin is "an exaggeration or diminishment of what God created us to be."[10] In your fallen psychology, you are prone either to exaggerate (what Romans 12 has in view) or to diminish reality, and your fallen psychology impacts much more than how you esteem yourself. In a sense, all sinful actions are psychological in nature. Thinking precedes most of our sins, and most of our sins are committed consciously. Fallen psychology leads to fallen actions. So it's important that you understand your tendencies. You need to know how you tend to see the world, process the world, and present yourself.

Plus, you are going to be confronting fallen psychologies other than your own; namely, the people, communities, and cultures that you are planting within. Most of the time, you are going to be dealing with people who are very ignorant of who they are and who are unwilling to change who they are. You have to work at taking the log out of your own eye, if you are going to have any chance of treating the speck in your neighbor's eye.

We believe that God the Holy Spirit's job is to lead us into all truth, and that truth is about who God is, and who we are in relationship to our God. We come to the conviction that we are sinners and need God's grace because the Holy Spirit makes us aware. You cannot change until you have become conscious of the need to change. Self-awareness is the issue. I contend that most church planters are ignorant of who they are, how they perceive, how they process, and how they present to others. A lot of planters live in a false reality. There is the real them created in the image of God, and then there is the distorted them—exaggerated or diminished—that they have cultivated or fueled in their own psychological mess. It is the distorted them that they present to the world and to others.

In an effort to grow in self-awareness, I use a tool called the Enneagram. The Enneagram is not your typical self awareness tool where you punch in a bunch of info and then it tells you, "This is who you are and these are the types of jobs you should have." The Enneagram is very holistic and complex. The best thing about it, when properly understood and administered, is that it causes you to ask questions that you probably never would have asked. When you begin to ask these types of questions the door to self-awareness opens. At my church, we have a rule that you can't serve in a leadership position unless you and your wife have been Enneagram-ed and it has been a huge blessing to us.

Seeking self-awareness will deliver you from a lot of drama. If you know who you are, you are going to be able to escape a lot of the temptations in planting—especially relational ones. Most relational problems are caused by a lack of self awareness. We know that the Church promotes a gospel of relationship with God and relationship with others. Your growth in relationship with God and others is going to happen as you put to death your ignorance and resistance to change. This is the battleground. Make sure you are always investigating your self-awareness. Always be dealing with yourself and your psychology. Always ask yourself hard questions. Your success is going to come down to what you do with your ignorance and unwillingness to change.

35

DISABILITY

If your church plant doesn't include people with disabilities, your church is *disobedient* and will be disabled itself.[11]

36

JESUS'S NUMBERS

Think about the ministry of Jesus. He identified and recruited twelve disciples who were with Him throughout the duration of His three-year ministry. Through these years, hundreds and thousands periodically were served and ministered to by Jesus and the Twelve. But! They weren't consistent followers like the Twelve were. Then at the end of Jesus' life, one of the Twelve betrays him, ten of the Twelve forsake Him, and when He died only one of the Twelve was near the cross with a group of women (If you want to know who is going to stick by your side in your ministry, it is probably going to be the women in your church.).

The point is that, numerically, there were very few committed followers of Jesus in His life. This should shape your own expectations and take some weight off your shoulders. The masses will come and go. That is what they do. When you go through numerical ups and down, don't fret—Jesus went through that too. Sometimes crowds were enamored with Jesus and followed Him, and sometimes Jesus fed thousands. Other times whole villages begged Him to leave and whole groups of people plotted to kill Him. Don't get wrapped up in your church's numbers, get wrapped up in the fact that you go through all of the fluctuations *with Him*.

37

CHURCH PLANTING IN HARD PLACES

Hard places are wherever people live. But some places are harder to plant in than others. Some of you are going to plant in harder places. Planting among the poor, the marginalized and those impacted by systemic sociological issues brings unique challenges. Here are some things for you to consider if, you are planting in this type of context:

It's going to be slow. Everything will be slow. Forget about getting your vision/mission done in three years in these situations. It might take you three years to build a foundation, to see doors open for the gospel, and to gain the trust of the community. Search the Scriptures and see for yourself that most of God's greatest works took time. We all long for a ministry of miracles because it fixes things fast, but they are rare in God's redemptive activity. Plan on the long haul. If you are planting in a hard place in America, you should adopt an international missions approach in terms of a timeline. When we do missions and church planting overseas, we go in knowing it's going to be a long ride. Take a deep breath and trust God. He will build His Church.

You must recognize your limitations. When you plant in hard places needs, will be everywhere. Because you have a heart to help you will want to meet all of them. But, you have limitations. Even Jesus had a time when He fed no one else, healed no one else, and left people in need. Do you trust God enough to walk away from a need? Some of you have a big heart and a little capacity. You have a great desire to meet hundreds of needs, but you only have the resources, gifts, and character to meet the needs of ten. Know this and embrace it or you will burnt out quickly.

Don't let needs distract you from the mission. You know what's amazing? Jesus met so many needs and yet never allowed the meeting of need to cause mission drift. Jesus was with the marginalized, the poor, and those impacted by systemic oppression, and yet managed to develop the Twelve! It wasn't an either-or for Him. Those enmeshed in their needs will not like that you are on mission. They won't see the relationship between mission and meeting needs. You will feel immense pressure to respond to the immediate at the expense of obedience and the eternal welfare of souls.

Learn about the community. Most of you who are going to plant in a hard place are walking into a situation where you are ignorant of what's going on in that community. Don't quote me demographic statistics or studies to show that you know people. People are more than statistics. It takes time to learn and know a community, and this is done best in person. Getting to know your community will help you to contextualize the gospel, which will result in a more effective way of applying it to people. You have two ears and one mouth for a reason: God wants you to listen more than talk.

Get a job. If you can't raise ten years' worth of funding then get a job that pays well and allows you to plant when you can. Like I've said, you will either worry about money or ministry—your choice. Some bivocational planters have actually found greater credibility and receptivity from their community because they are seen as normal. Listen, offerings and tithes aren't going to be much in areas of poverty. If you are on a one- or three-year timeline as a church plant, where you are expected to be able to support yourselves in that time, it's probably not going to happen.

Remember that there is glory in hard places. Jesus was born in a manger. It's natural for those of us on the outside of a hard place to only see one aspect of that place—it's hardness. When you come into hard places you will be confronted by the glory of God. God is at work. He has already worked. Honestly, when I moved to Baltimore, I went through some shock because a lot of my perspective on the city was formed by *The Wire,* the news, studies, demographics and sensational marketing designed to induce compassion and to get people to move here. However, when I moved here, I was brought to tears by the glory of God in this city that was already here, and had been here for hundreds of years. When you come into a hard place, be on the lookout for the wealth, gifts, ingenuity, resilience, brilliance, and favor that God has already given to it.

Don't underestimate the importance of preaching! If you can't preach well, don't go to a hard place.

People want to go to church in hard places. It's usually a respite and blessing, and typically it's embedded in the culture's mindset already. A lot of people go into hard places and want to hang out, afraid to start church services too soon. This is a mistake in most cases. People want to go to church, so start your church; worship, pray, take communion, baptize, preach, fellowship, and bring people to the throne of grace.

Be honest about who you are and where you are going to plant. Can we have an honest, open, and humble conversation about a white guy planting in a predominantly black neighborhood? Can we have a conversation about the challenges we as planters face because we plant in neighborhoods that aren't ours? Can we talk about the way we show up thinking people are seeing Jesus in us, and all they see is us at first? Can we talk about how our personalities—the way we perceive, process and present—play into planting in hard places? Can we assess whether or not a person is uniquely qualified, gifted and called to go to a hard place? Can we talk about the systemic racism, poverty, classism, economic pressures, health issues, and violence that often besets these communities, and the impact all these will have on the planter and the plant? We need to.

Spend some time studying, meditating, and figuring out how to apply Isaiah 61 to your hard place.

Know that your labor is not in vain, if you are in a hard place. Redwoods take hundreds of years to grow. Good wine is refined over time. Most of the great things that God has done have been done over time and in hard places. You are making a difference; you will make a difference. May the grace and peace of God be with you.

38

MYTHOLOGY AND CHURCH PLANTING

Myth #1: You are not an obstacle to church planting
Myth #2: You have to have a big church
Myth #3: You need to be able to send a lot of people
Myth #4: You have to have a lot of money
Myth #5: You need to be unique to do it
Myth #6: It's going to hurt your church
Myth #7: There are already a lot of churches and the harvest isn't plentiful
Myth #8: I have limited resources so I can't do anything
Myth #9: You can plant a church without plans and others
Myth #10: Prayer doesn't have to be your primary strategy

In reality all you need is three things to participate in planting a church:

. . . a willingness to join Jesus as he's building his church,
. . . a called gifted and qualified man who has been assessed
     and affirmed by a local church, and
. . . a small group of people committed to seeing the gospel
     shared and disciples made.

39

WORKING ON IT VERSUS WORKING IN IT

The first time I heard this concept was at a church planting conference with the president of the Acts 29 Network. The big idea is simple. You need to spend time working on your plant: planning, dreaming, strategizing, thinking, organizing. Picture your plant as a car that needs work. It needs to be brought in and put on the lift and examined, then assessed, and then work needs to be done. You can't just continue to drive it without working on it or you will eventually put it in a place where something's irreparable. Planters usually spend time working on the plant until launch then they work *in* the plant and usually don't spend much time working *on* it. This leads to ceilings, frustrations, and hindrances to growth. You will need to set aside time to work on your plant.

You will have to be intentional about this. The daily needs of the plant will plead with you to work in the church and not on it. It will indeed be necessary to spend time working in your plant: preaching, teaching, overseeing, pastoring, counseling, meeting, leading, etc. Planters usually have a bent or a desire for one of these over the other. You have to be aware of this, so that you can ask others to look after the part you don't like to or aren't gifted in. You will find that working in and on will ebb and flow with the seasons and growth of your plant. At times, one will need more of your attention than the other. Sometimes it's similar to a tennis match, where they go back and forth in the life of the church plant.

A good illustration of working on and in is found in Acts 6. Due to the growth of the church, a problem arose that required work both on and in the church. The Apostles made a decision to work on the church, and addressed the problem by bringing seven men on to work in the church. Brothers, see to it that you are paying attention to both of these needs.

40

PARENTING

Few things have impacted you as much as the way you were or were not parented. Parenting influences pastoring and planting. There a lot of parallels between planting and parenting. We tend to pastor and plant in the same way that we have experienced parenting. So, it's important to be aware of how you were parented; for most planters that's where they learned how to do relationships, and planting is highly relational.

There are going to be some people in your plant that need parenting. In fact, a lot of people in the culture and context you're trying to reach have not been properly parented. They've been abused, they've been detached, they haven't been looked after, and part of what they're looking for in your church plant is a parent. Don't be surprised if the door to a person's soul is the parent they never had or the one they need right now. But here's the sad truth: you're not going to be able to parent everybody. Even if you raise up other leaders, you're probably not going to be able to carry the parental load that many expect of you. Like Jesus when He was on Earth, you have limitations. You cannot make up every deficit of parenting in every person's life. Be faithful and do what you can and leave the rest to the Father, Son, and Spirit, and the body of Christ.

It is more important for you to be a good parent than a great planter. These two don't have to be opposed to each other, but at times you have to choose one over the other. As a general rule, always choose your family. Many church planters send monthly and quarterly reports about how many evangelistic opportunities they have had, how many baptisms they had, how many people are attending church on Sunday, and so on and so forth. *Brothers, we need to make sure that our parenting report is always superior to our planting report.*

Investing in your wife and children is more important than investing in your plant. *1 Timothy 3:5 functions as a thermometer for us to measure whether or not we can plant and pastor—also once we are planting, how well we are doing.*

Finally, parenting will teach you a lot about planting. In fact, it's going to teach you a lot of painful things about yourself. In the end it will help you to become a better planter, if you keep your mind, heart and soul open to what God wants to show you.

41

DEPRESSION

Depression is real for church planters. It's something that a lot of us are dealing with. It's unfortunate that so many people are in denial about this. Dismissing or denying this does not make it go away. Depression can be found in the Scriptures, and there are many people in the Bible who struggled with depression. God has a purpose for depression. It is not wasted in your life. He can and will use it to accomplish His pleasure and purpose in your life.

Church planters are particularly exposed and vulnerable to depression. The volatility and the transient nature of things when we plant contribute to depression. Also, planting has a unique way of excavating the past, which is often very painful as we are trying to plant a new church. This tends to cultivate depression as well.

There is nothing wrong with you if you're battling this. It's normal. In fact, you're probably in the majority, and those who don't deal with depression as church planters are in the minority. There are some good books on depression, but few rival Dr. Martin Lloyd-Jones' work on spiritual depression. The first chapter alone is worth the price, and it's one of those books that every planter should read annually. In the book, he speaks of the concept of talking to yourself. Depression can be catalyzed and cultivated by what we say to ourselves. We must always remember that the most powerful influence in our lives is the voice no one hears but you.

Depression is not exclusively brought on by self talk. There are external causes and circumstances that bring it on. There are also intrinsic causes embedded in us that are much harder to understand. No matter what the source of our depression, we must learn how to cope and how to deal with it. We must learn how to gospel ourselves—and to be quite frank, we must learn how to preach to ourselves. Church planters are often the worst at listening to their own messages, and those of us who battle depression can't afford not to learn the art and science of speaking the truth in love to ourselves. I've said it before and I'll say it again, the most powerful influence in your life is the voice that no one hears but you.

I want to encourage you to press into your relationship with God in deeper and more intentional ways. Make time to do this. If you struggle with depression you are going to need more time with God than the person who doesn't. You are going to need to find places where you can connect with the Lord. Your normal routines may need to be upended and changed in order to ensure you get what you need in your relationship with God. Prayer is your lifeline in times of depression. Whatever you do, keep praying. Reading the Bible is important, but, in my opinion, prayer is more important. A depressed person needs a relationship with God more than anything else, and prayer is highly relational in nature.

When we are depressed we aren't going to want to do some of the things that will help us. This is normal. This is also why I think all depressed people should try to do things every day that they don't want to do, like exercise. Depressed people need to know how to do things when they don't feel like it. We need to train our bodies and minds, that some things are just right and need to be done even when they feel wrong or unattractive.

Unfortunately, treating depression is subject to exaggeration and diminishment. This means some people are going to lean too far in one direction or the other. We should have a holistic approach since we are embodied souls. Depression is complex. If there was an easy and quick fix, we would all know it. As a general rule, treating depression requires patience, reasonable expectations, and endurance. The gains are typically small and the progress is usually incremental. Don't be discouraged, brothers; most great things grow slow!

Should you see a counselor about your depression? Yes, particularly if it is regularly interrupting your ability to do God's will. Should you take medicine for your depression? This decision should be made in consultation with your doctors, counselors, wife, parents, pastors, and trusted friends.

One of the best things to have in your life to help you with depression is a good friend. A brother that you can trust. I mean *really* trust. This means you don't hesitate to share your deepest, and, at times, darkest thoughts and feelings with him. One of the reasons that some of us need counseling is that we don't have this person in our lives. It's better to go to counseling and receive this than to sit alone without it. A good friend can help you navigate through your valley of the shadow of death. A good friend is a good listener. They listen more than they talk. A good friend will make you feel heard and understood.

42

A RIGHT VIEW OF WOMEN

What do you feel when you look at a woman? What do you think? What does your gut tell you? The answer to these questions reveal whether or not you are perceiving women the way God wants you. You are going to minister, to serve, disciple, and love women as a church planter. There's no getting around this. So, you'd better have a right view of them, because how you view a person dictates how you treat them.

First, a woman is created in the image of God. Nothing ever erases this fact. Not her looks, dress, actions, social or economic status, ethnicity, education, or vocation. She is irrevocably human first and foremost. A failure to see women like this first leads to all kinds of ill-treatment of women. Racism and gender prejudice share a false presupposition; namely, that the individual in view is something other than an image-bearer. We have to be careful as planters to uphold this truth. If we don't, we will find ourselves making room for the flesh, and the result will be that women in our plants are not treasured and treated with honor, respect, and love.

Second, a woman who is a Christian is a daughter of God because of the gospel. They are part of the family, redeemed and rescued by His grace by virtue of the life, death, and resurrection of Jesus. This is what we should see before we see anything else.

Third, a woman is either a mother, sister or wife according to Scripture. In 1 Timothy 5:2 Paul tells Timothy to treat "older women as mothers, younger women as sisters, in all purity." He assigns us a way to think about women. We aren't left to our own depraved minds when it comes to how we should perceive women.

Attractive women will visit your church plant. Count on it. The issue is, how will you handle this? Let me tell you how you're going to handle it: according to your perception of that attractive woman. This is why your perceptions have to be shaped by Scripture and not fear, worldliness, or the opinions of men.

When it comes to women, let us avoid the error of licentiousness and also the error of segregation.

43

----

10 CONSIDERATIONS ABOUT SLEEP

1. Sleep deprivation is a national epidemic that impacts church planting.
2. Sleep is vital to your health and you need it more than you think.
3. There is a theology of sleep in the Bible. You should know it, study it, and then teach and preach on it.
4. Church planting is one of many sleep killers.
5. There are things that can help you sleep. Find out what they are and use them wisely.
6. There are different types of sleep. Planters need the deep type in order to attain rest and restoration.
7. The place, position, and environment you sleep in matters. If you are having trouble sleeping, attempt to adjust these to see if it makes a difference.
8. You might need to intentionally plan for and organize your daily sleep.
9. Sleep is an act of worship and one of the greatest demonstration of faith.
10. Jesus slept.

44

----

12 THOUGHTS ON FUNDRAISING

1. You are going to have to deal with your unsanctified thoughts, feelings, and theology about money before you fundraise, or it will bite you.
2. You have to deal with shame, fear, and guilt. These three emotions ruin fundraising for most planters.
3. You have to be personally committed to giving to the cause that you are asking your people and others to give to.
4. You need to make your fiscal picture clear and easy to understand.
5. You need to make giving easy, targeted, and full of purpose.
6. You should preach and teach on money and giving annually.
7. You need to have a short-term memory in order to deal with the refusals you are going to receive when you ask for money.
8. You should keep your proposals short and to the point; the longer something is the better it has to be.
9. You should try to get people to your site, area, city, or church facility before you make your pitch. There's something about exercising the five senses during a pitch that's more effective.
10. You should avoid these two extremes: begging and seeming like you have everything you need.

11. You should build relationships; these produce the best results in fundraising.
12. You should get your church giving to your network, denomination, and other churches right off the bat—even if it's the metaphorical widow's mite.

45

ME TOO

Let's get something straight. Rapists should be put to death. The church should seek justice in cases of sexual assault, and not hide behind distorted views of grace, mercy, and love. This is true for men who assault women, women who assault men, or any other situation. God is not partial. Justice shouldn't cater to one gender over another. The guilty should face justice. The thief on the cross was forgiven and would see Jesus, but he still died on the cross. Christians need to let this sink deep down into their thoughts.

A church planter should have no tolerance for unwanted sexual advances in the church. Unfortunately, we have to be on the lookout for serial sexual predators. They can thrive in the church if we let them. It is one thing to struggle with sexual sin, but it is an entirely different thing to live in patterns of unrepentant, unwanted sexual advances. It's critical that we report the sexual assaults to the authorities! A failure to do so shows that a man is unfit to lead and plant a church. In the best case, we want the guilty parties to cooperate as we pursue civil justice with a spirit of humility, repentance, and hope.

Beyond the legal problem, there is the problem of dealing with sexual assault pastorally. There are so many variables that need to be considered before making a decision. (By the way, this is another reason why you shouldn't plant alone.) I'd advise seeking wise counsel, meaning don't talk to anyone under fifty about it and make sure you consult people who are familiar with both sound ecclesiology and the law. As a general rule the victim should be allowed to stay in the church if they desire, and the person who assaulted them probably needs to leave. It is what it is. Also, this is why I recommend you have a discipline policy in place when you launch one, that all members agree to.

The world won't like what I'm about to say, especially in the #MeToo era, but there is still hope for those who have committed the sin and crime of sexual assault. There is forgiveness, mercy, and love to be found in the gospel. We have to be wise in our application of all this, but it doesn't negate that God is love.

Sexual assault is birthed in an idolatrous heart, and in a mind that refuses to see a woman as anything other than a sexual object. As a church planter, you have to make sure you combat this in practice, preaching, and discipleship. If you can't look a woman in the eye when you talk to her there's something wrong. If you can't talk to a woman that's attractive within appropriate times and venues, do us all a favor and don't plant a church.

46

FUN!

You'd better have fun planting your church. There is an ocean of joy to experience in church planting. There are so many things that will bring you joy, and there is so much fun to be had. As violent, volatile, and challenging as it is, church planting is a virtual Disneyland of ecclesiological providences for you as a church planter. At the end of the day, you get to plant a church. You could be doing a lot of other things with your life, and if God called you to plant a church then God actually told you to do something—and that is really cool. That God would tell you to do something—and that He would resource it and support it with unmistakable workings of the Spirit—should be a joy-sparking reality. Plus, the funnest thing on the planet is doing God's will. We know that church planting is part of God's will and consequently, if you are obeying God in the process, you should expect to have some serious fun doing it.

The problem you are going to face is that fun is hard for the flesh. The flesh is prone to miss or deny the reality that planting a church is fun. But that doesn't change the reality—church planting *is* fun. Here is the bottom line: if you're not having fun planting your church, you need to repent. If you're not having fun you're basically saying that your missiological endeavor is devoid of any blessings or providences that would produce joy and pleasure, and I refuse to believe that.

As a general rule, God places providential blessings in our lives. Jesus' life was the only life ever lived on the planet in which you could logically argue that there should not have been any joy. As Isaiah said, He was a "man of sorrows" (Isaiah 53:3 NASB). But the Bible says that Jesus, "for the joy that was set before him endured the cross, despising the shame, and is seated at the right hand of the throne of God." (Hebrews 12:2). If Jesus could have joy in establishing the Church through death, abandonment, and slander, then you can find joy in planting your lowercase church.

Somewhere along the way, many planters lose the joy in church planting. Sure, you are going to have some of depression and weariness, but if it is never fun . . . ever . . . and you never experience any seasons of joy . . . then I cannot believe that is God's doing.

So, what's at the heart of this? Why don't we find planting to be fun? Here are my top five reasons:

1. We don't really know God's character.

2. We don't really trust God.

3. Our identity is not in Christ, it's in being a church planter.

4. We refuse to acknowledge God's blessings and refuse to bring our flesh into submission to God by taking it by the throat and saying, "We're going to praise God and have some fun!"

5. We believe that we must have instant success and never make mistakes.

Overcoming those five pitfalls will not be easy. You will . . . you will . . . you will have to fight to have fun. As John 10:10 says, "The thief comes only to steal and kill and destroy. I came that they may have life and have it abundantly." This is the dynamic reality you live within. Your life and joy are under siege and you must fight the battle for your joy with all the grace that God supplies. You are going to face the temptation to feel that everything is morose in your life and your ministry. And if you're not willing to fight to have fun then eventually you will succumb to the flesh's pull towards melancholy. It is a heavyweight fight for joy, and if you're not alert, your joy will get knocked out. The tempter wants to rob you of all fun in planting and is in constant pursuit of joy's destruction.

But no matter how powerful his lies are, it doesn't change the reality that there are some incredibly fun things in church planting. The unknown is exciting. The miraculous is exciting. The progress is exciting. Seeing God save people is exciting. Seeing lives transformed is exciting. Don't tell me that there is nothing exhilarating in church planting! You've got to keep looking for these things and celebrating them.

One of the implications of all this talk about fun is that there should be a lot of laughter in your plant. A lot of planters don't know how to laugh at themselves, their people, their church, their plans, or much of anything at all. They are so serious. They act like their plans came down from Mount Sinai and that

God wrote them on the wall with His hand Daniel 5-style. What you are doing is important, but it's not that serious. We need to ask ourselves the Joker's question in *The Dark Knight:* "Why so serious?" Maybe you need to put up his face and that question at your desk to remind you of that. You do need to work hard and be faithful, but you also need to be able to esteem yourself and your efforts humbly. You are still a sinner prone to wandering and prone to error. An excessive and solemn seriousness about your ministry is really just a manifestation of pride. At the end of the day, you are a servant who has been called by God to go plant a church—and that is fun.

Some things in church planting you have to convert from solemnity to fun. It's probably going to be your propensity as a planter to be overly serious and to zap things of their fun. As you are leading your people and implementing initiatives, be aware of how you can have fun doing it. As a planter you should talk about fun openly and publicly. Always tell your people what your vision is. Tell them how you are going to make disciples, plant churches, and transform neighborhoods. But be sure to tell them—always tell them—that you are going to have fun doing every bit of it. Just as in Psalm 103, the phrase "Praise the Lord, my soul" needs to be on repeat in your life and church. You have to learn to talk to yourself and remind yourself of the joy of the Lord. You have to learn to convert things in your church and in your life into opportunities for fun and opportunities to praise God.

Finally, don't let planting kill you. Don't be that guy who was having a lot of fun and was a joyful follower of Jesus, and then went into the ministry and three years later hates God, doesn't want to be married, doesn't even want to be part of a church, and wishes he had never heard the term church planting. There are some men that have been tragically beaten up by church planting. What we should do, and often don't, is nurse those men. We need to get better at that. But honestly, a lot of us are just wimps. For most of us, if we really consider the stuff that we are down about, it becomes clear that our sadness is totally disproportionate to our reality. There are real atrocities in this world and real piercing pains that people experience. In the context of these, you not knowing where you are going to meet next Sunday is not that big of a deal. You not knowing if your offering is going to be $2,000 or $3,000 is not that big of a deal. It may feel like it, but it's not.

Again, you've got to fight for your joy. If you aren't willing to fight for it then sometime during your church planting experience the violence and volatility of planting is going to rob you of your joy—it can "kill" you. I'd love to see a generation of planters who are sober, honest, and can live in seasons of depression because of the gospel, but who have some incredible fun while they are planting.

God can handle all of your failures and mistakes. When you fail you are going to feel like it's all over—but it's not all over! *The world will not end and God's purposes will not be thwarted because of your church planting mishaps.* What does the Bible say about Jesus right now? He is sitting at the right hand of the Father. He is not wringing His hands with anxiety. He is sitting. Jesus is the sovereign King and you are just one of His servants. So, go have some fun following Him and being an ambassador on His behalf!

Grace and peace,
Michael Crawford

47

ENDNOTES

1. Roger, P.C. and L. Vischer, eds. *The Fourth World Conference on Faith and Order: Montreal 1963.* London: SCM Press, 1964.

2. "Mr. Spurgeon as a Literary Man," in *The Autobiography of Charles H. Spurgeon, Compiled from His Letters, Diaries, and Records by His Wife and Private Secretary,* vol. 4, 1878–1892. Curtis & Jennings, 1900. p. 268.

3. "What's the size of U.S. Churches?" Hartford Institute for Religion Research. Accessed May 16 2017. http://hirr.hartsem.edu/research/fastfacts/fast_facts.html#sizecong.

4. Spurgeon, Charles H. *Lectures To My Students.* Kindle Edition, p. 26–27.

5. Murphy-O'Connor, Jerome. *Saint Paul's Corinth: Texts and Archaeology.* Collegeville, MN: Liturgical Press, 2002. p. 177–182.

6. "Are more women enrolling in seminary?" Hartford Institute for Religion Research. Accessed May 16, 2017. http://hirr.hartsem.edu/research/fastfacts/fast_facts.html#womenin

7. This number was calculated based on 2014 data from the US Census Bureau and the US Bureau of Labor Statistics.

8. Seltzer, Edward, and Warren Bird. "The State of Church Planting in the United States: Research Overview and Qualitative Study of Primary Church Planting Entities." *Christianity Today.* Accessed May 16, 2017. www.christianitytoday.com/assets/10228.pdf

9. The Cross Movement. "Cypha the Next Day" (song). 1999.

10. This definition is taken from an unreleased publication by Crosspoint Ministries on the Enneagram.

11. The thought behind this assertion can be attributed to Nathan Grills and was part of his presentation on disability inclusion in India at the 2016 CCIH Conference in Baltimore, Maryland.

48

ABOUT MIKE

Michael Crawford is a pastor and author. A native of the L.A. area, Michael graduated from Crossroads High School in Santa Monica and briefly attended UCLA before God reached into his heart and changed his life forever. He transferred to The Master's College where he earned a BA in Political Science and a Master's of Divinity from The Master's Seminary.

Michael pastored Free Grace Church in the Antelope Valley, California, from 1997–2008. In 1999, Michael felt a tremendous burden for the sanctity of human life, and subsequently became the cofounder and president of Care Net Women's Resource Center of North County from 1999–2008. He served on the staff of Cornerstone Bible Church, Ridgecrest, California, as church planting and missions pastor 2008–2009.

In 2006, Michael also launched Innovative Consulting, a nonprofit consulting business for the Antelope Valley's underserved community. He wrote *100 Meditations: An Everyday Book for Everyday People* in 2008, and in 2009 Michael was called to Baltimore, Maryland, where he planted Freedom Church. This was fueled by his passion to pastor in an urban city with racial diversity, and to pour his knowledge and experience into the lives of African American men. Currently he is the state director of missions for the Baptist Convention of Maryland.

Michael has been married for twenty years to Dani and has five children: Claudia, Tabitha, Nehemiah, Keturah, and Ezra. In addition to being a triathlete, his favorite pastimes include dating his wife, being a 'sugar daddy' to his kids, golf, and cycling. *MichaelCrawfordsBlog.com*

BOOKS FOR CONTRARIAN SAINTS

The Beginning: A Second Look at the First Sin

"[A] very readable and engaging discussion on the nature and consequences of the original sin using the biblical accounts as his primary authority … A sound background in scripture, a solid presentation of his positions, and generous application make this book a very good reference on the subject." —*The American Journal of Biblical Theology*

Deeper Magic: The Theology Behind the Writings of C.S. Lewis

"… a treasure trove of systematized information—a must for every C.S. Lewis fan, and all the rest of us who should be."—Norman Geisler, PhD

Intruding Upon the Timeless: Meditations on Art, Faith, and Mystery

"A collection of brief essays by the editor of *Image,* a distinguished journal of religion and the arts. A nice mix of the whimsical, provocative, and devout, as befits the variegated subject."—*First Things*

Revealed: A Storybook Bible for Grown-Ups

"*Revealed* sets out to crush any notion that the Bible is a safe, inspirational read. Instead the artwork here, historic and contemporary, takes a warts-and-all approach to even the most troubling passages, trading well-meaning elision for unvarnished truth."
—J. Mark Bertrand, novelist, speaker, and founder of the Bible Design Blog

A Book for Hearts & Minds: What You Should Read and Why

"Curators of the imagination, stewards of the tradition, priests of print, [Hearts & Minds Bookstore has] always done more than sold books: they have furnished faithful minds and hearts. This book is a lovely testimony to that good work."
—James K.A. Smith, Calvin College, author of *You Are What You Love: The Spiritual Power of Habit*

Godly Character(s): Insights for Spiritual Passion from the Lives of Eight Women in the Bible

"Our love for Christ and our willingness to follow Him by letting Him shape, form, and mold our character at the level of daily habits and practices is a way that every believer made in His image (women and men) proclaims His love to a world gone mad."
—Robert William Alexander, author of *The Gospel-Centered Life at Work*

Good Posture: Engaging Current Culture with Ancient Faith

"I couldn't recommend this book more highly. Please read it cover to cover. Please share it. And please, for the love of God, start living it."
—Scott Sauls, senior pastor of Christ Presbyterian Church (Nashville) and author of *Jesus Outside the Lines*

LEARN MORE AT SQUAREHALOBOOKS.COM